Dart By Example

Design and develop modern web applications with Google's bold and productive language through engaging example projects

Davy Mitchell

PUBLISHING

BIRMINGHAM - MUMBAI

Dart By Example

First published: September 2015

Production reference: 1220915

Published by Packt Publishing Ltd.
Livery Place
35 Livery Street
Birmingham B3 2PB, UK.

ISBN 978-1-78528-247-8

www.packtpub.com

Credits

Author
Davy Mitchell

Reviewers
Aristides Villarreal Bravo

Claudio d'Angelis

Joris Hermans

Jana Moudrá

Commissioning Editor
Veena Pagare

Acquisition Editors
Vinay Argekar

Richard Brookes-Bland

Content Development Editor
Athira Laji

Technical Editor
Rohan Uttam Gosavi

Copy Editor
Neha Vyas

Project Coordinator
Harshal Ved

Proofreader
Safis Editing

Indexer
Mariammal Chettiyar

Production Coordinator
Conidon Miranda

Cover Work
Conidon Miranda

About the Author

Davy Mitchell is a software developer with over 17 years of commercial experience in many varied industries. He started out in the world of C++ and progressed through the dot-com boom to the Microsoft.com era and into .Net, SQL Server, and other web technologies.

In the past few years, he has worked on software installation, continuous integration, build automation, and tooling, while also developing frontend interfaces. Davy is passionate about both developer productivity and moving web applications forward. He enjoys exploring new technologies, platforms, and open source, using Linux and Windows operating systems.

He writes news, features, and book reviews on Dart at `www.divingintodart.com`, and demo projects that are shared on GitHub, covering HTML5 and even Minecraft. He regularly takes part in the week-long Python game jam, PyWeek, and maintains Chocolatey packages for Dart on the Windows platform. When taking a break from coding, he enjoys cycling, loom knitting, gardening, and retrogaming.

I would like to thank my wife, Marta, and my sons, Niall, Jamie, and Alex, for their invaluable support and patience as I worked on this book. I would also like to thank the many individuals who helped me at each step of the creation of this book. Finally, I would like to thank the Dart team for creating an outstanding language.

About the Reviewers

Aristides Villarreal Bravo is a Java developer and member of the NetBeans Dream Team and Java User Groups. He lives in Panamá. He has organized and participated in various conferences and seminars related to Java, JavaEE, NetBeans, the NetBeans platform, free software, and mobile devices, both nationally and internationally. He is a writer of many tutorials and blogs about Java, NetBeans, and web developers. He has reviewed several books for *Packt Publishing*. He is also a developer of plugins for NetBeans. He is a specialist in JSE, JEE, JPA, Agile, and Continuous Integration. He shares his knowledge at his blog, `http://avbravo.blogspot.com`.

I would like to thank my family.

Claudio d'Angelis is an Italian programmer with more than 10 years of experience in document digitization, web development, and Linux administration. As an early adopter of Dart, he still continues to contribute to this community. His contributions include writing articles, working on open source projects, and speaking at conferences.

Joris Hermans is a developer with a lot of passion for the Web, innovation, and new technologies. He has general knowledge of many tools, languages, and platforms. He is the proud owner of a lot of Dart packages, a real-time Dart framework called force, a search engine named Bounty Hunter, a persistent abstraction layer called cargo, a dependency injection for Dart called wired, and many more. Joris also likes to speak about the Web and Dart, so it is possible that you will meet him at conferences.

Jana Moudrá is a passionate developer, teacher, and modern Web and mobile technologies evangelist. She created her first web page at the age of 10. At that time, she had no idea what her future field of expertise would be. Later on, she became interested in technologies such as JavaScript and jQuery, but finally ended up with Dart. She has been exploring it since Milestone 2 (M2). She is also interested in the areas of user experience, design, and Android app development. Jana cofounded the company Juicymo, where she works on juicy apps and products. When she is not working, she organizes developer-related events on her favorite technologies for the Czech developers community and regularly speaks at conferences. You can visit her company's website at `http://www.juicymo.com`.

www.PacktPub.com

Support files, eBooks, discount offers, and more

For support files and downloads related to your book, please visit www.PacktPub.com.

Did you know that Packt offers eBook versions of every book published, with PDF and ePub files available? You can upgrade to the eBook version at www.PacktPub.com and as a print book customer, you are entitled to a discount on the eBook copy. Get in touch with us at service@packtpub.com for more details.

At www.PacktPub.com, you can also read a collection of free technical articles, sign up for a range of free newsletters and receive exclusive discounts and offers on Packt books and eBooks.

https://www2.packtpub.com/books/subscription/packtlib

Do you need instant solutions to your IT questions? PacktLib is Packt's online digital book library. Here, you can search, access, and read Packt's entire library of books.

Why subscribe?

- Fully searchable across every book published by Packt
- Copy and paste, print, and bookmark content
- On demand and accessible via a web browser

Free access for Packt account holders

If you have an account with Packt at www.PacktPub.com, you can use this to access PacktLib today and view 9 entirely free books. Simply use your login credentials for immediate access.

Table of Contents

Preface

The Web is undoubtedly a great platform for applications, and it continues to develop at a rapid pace. The software development tools have progressed too, but some technologies seem unsuited to modern demands. Most web developers spend a good deal of time researching the current state of tools and libraries.

I discovered Dart when I wanted to write an HTML5 application and wanted to try out one of the many new web languages everyone was talking about. I chanced upon Dart and was soon hooked on the language and platform. Being able to compile a client-side application before loading it in a web browser was life changing! There were great tools and features available, and it was updated almost every week.

After learning Dart, I soon started a blog on it and enjoyed showcasing the language with some fun colorful demos, news, and reviews, learning new aspects to blog about. The community was great to interact with, and when the opportunity came to write this book, I knew I had to do it. I find working with the Dart programming language more enjoyable than any other language. I hope you have this experience too, and write some great applications.

This book is designed to give you a clear picture of Dart's capabilities so that you are able to evaluate its suitability for a task and are ready to approach the design of a solution. We will be looking at Dart in a variety of projects, which will be, hopefully, close to the real-world applications that you will end up writing.

What this book covers

Chapter 1, *Starting the Text Editor*, will make you familiar with the background of the language, the development tools, and how to run your first Dart application.

Chapter 2, *Advancing the Editor*, explores classes, data structures, how to build a user interface, and how to use the HTML5 canvas. Furthermore, it looks at how to compile the text editor to JavaScript.

Chapter 3, Slideshow Presentations, covers more advanced class features, such as mixins, string processing, and event handling, while describing how to build a web-based presentation package.

Chapter 4, Language, Motion, and Sound, demonstrates a user interface localization and shows you how to use Dart for animation and sound effects in the presentation package.

Chapter 5, A Blog Server, shows you how to write server-side code in Dart, how to handle a text file, how to serve web pages, and how to deploy on different operating systems. It concludes with benchmarking the server using Dart itself.

Chapter 6, Blog Server Advanced, goes deeper into the server application request processing to populate access logs, file handling, form handling, and security. JSON and XML are covered using Dart packages, as is the powerful asynchronous operation support.

Chapter 7, Live Data Collection, kicks off the largest project in this book, an earthquake monitoring system. Dart will be used to collect real-world JSON data and store it in an industry-standard relational database.

Chapter 8, Live Data and a Web Service, improves the data collection and walks you through how to use Dart to create a RESTful web service. This service is then used to create a live data display using Dart in the web browser.

Chapter 9, A Real-Time Visualization, returns Dart to the client side of HTML5, using a canvas, geolocation, and desktop notifications to create an advanced web application.

Chapter 10, Reports and an API, completes the earthquake system, extending the REST API to handle data input and querying. A Dart reporting website is created, covering data charting and the export feature.

What you need for this book

A modern computer running Windows, Linux, or Mac OS will be sufficient to run the tools and programs in this book.

The details of the following and alternatives to WebStorm are discussed in *Chapter 1, Starting the Text Editor*:

- Dart SDK and Dartium (http://www.dartlang.org)
- WebStorm (https://www.jetbrains.com/webstorm/)

For the database project, we are using PostgreSQL and pgAdmin:

- PostgreSQL (http://www.postgresql.org/)
- pgAdmin (http://www.pgadmin.org/)

Who this book is for

If you are familiar with web development and are looking to learn, or even just evaluate, Dart as a multipurpose language, this book is for you. No familiarity with the Dart language is assumed. Existing Dart programmers can explore a range of application types and powerful packages that are demonstrated in a practical manner in this book.

Conventions

In this book, you will find a number of styles of text that distinguish between different kinds of information. Here are some examples of these styles, and an explanation of their meaning.

Code words in text, database table names, folder names, filenames, file extensions, pathnames, dummy URLs, user input, and Twitter handles are shown as follows: "The dart:io package is important for the server side."

A block of code is set as follows:

```
try {
  throw new Exception("We have a problem!");
} catch (exception, stackTrace) {
  log.severe("Something really bad.", exception, stackTrace);
}
```

New terms and **important words** are shown in bold. Words that you see on the screen, in menus or dialog boxes for example, appear in the text like this: " Refresh the web browser again and the most recent post on **Chicken Facts** will have gone."

Warnings or important notes appear in a box like this.

Tips and tricks appear like this.

Reader feedback

Feedback from our readers is always welcome. Let us know what you think about this book — what you liked or may have disliked. Reader feedback is important for us to develop titles that you really get the most out of.

To send us general feedback, simply send an e-mail to feedback@packtpub.com, and mention the book title via the subject of your message.

If there is a topic that you have expertise in and you are interested in either writing or contributing to a book, see our author guide on www.packtpub.com/authors.

Customer support

Now that you are the proud owner of a Packt book, we have a number of things to help you to get the most from your purchase.

Downloading the example code

You can download the example code files for all Packt books you have purchased from your account at http://www.packtpub.com. If you purchased this book elsewhere, you can visit http://www.packtpub.com/support and register to have the files e-mailed directly to you.

Errata

Although we have taken every care to ensure the accuracy of our content, mistakes do happen. If you find a mistake in one of our books — maybe a mistake in the text or the code — we would be grateful if you would report this to us. By doing so, you can save other readers from frustration and help us improve subsequent versions of this book. If you find any errata, please report them by visiting http://www.packtpub.com/submit-errata, selecting your book, clicking on the **errata submission form** link, and entering the details of your errata. Once your errata are verified, your submission will be accepted and the errata will be uploaded on our website, or added to any list of existing errata, under the Errata section of that title. Any existing errata can be viewed by selecting your title from http://www.packtpub.com/support.

Piracy

Piracy of copyright material on the Internet is an ongoing problem across all media. At Packt, we take the protection of our copyright and licenses very seriously. If you come across any illegal copies of our works, in any form, on the Internet, please provide us with the location address or website name immediately so that we can pursue a remedy.

Please contact us at copyright@packtpub.com with a link to the suspected pirated material.

We appreciate your help in protecting our authors, and our ability to bring you valuable content.

Questions

You can contact us at questions@packtpub.com if you are having a problem with any aspect of the book, and we will do our best to address it.

Starting the Text Editor

The rung of a ladder was never meant to rest upon, but only to hold a man's foot long enough to enable him to put the other somewhat higher.

– Thomas Huxley

Defining Dart

Dart is a language and platform for modern web applications that can run both in the web browser and on the server. The Dart language, tools, and API allow innovative, productive, enlightened, and talented developers (that's you!) to write scalable web applications that make the best of the modern Web.

With Dart, you can take a leap forward in web development and tooling. It is a clean, modern, yet familiar language syntax that runs on a platform created by the world's leading virtual machine experts.

Dart is run as an open source project with a defined process for enhancement proposals. It has flexible libraries with common documentation packaging, unit testing, and dependency resolution. The language became an ECMA standard in July of 2014, and does not require any plugin for end users to run as it is compiled to JavaScript.

If that is not enough, you can bring your existing HTML, CSS, JavaScript skills, and even code along for the ride—Dart plays nicely with others!

History of Web scripting

The high sophistication of current web pages with animations, dynamic content, fades, 3D effects, responsive designs, and clever navigation make it easy to forget that the early web was mostly textual pages, dumb forms, and images that often took a while to load. Then, along came JavaScript, in the form of a script interpreter built into the browser, providing form data validation, news ticker moving displays, animation, and games. For small projects, it succeeded in spicing up static websites without requiring server-side CGI scripts.

Developers enjoyed the near instant edit and refresh cycle—changing a line of code and hitting *F5* (**refresh**) in the browser to see the result. JavaScript did not stay in the browser and was soon found on the server side of web applications. It also became a general purpose script for use outside the browser.

 Fun fact: **JavaScript** was written in just ten days by Brendan Eich for the Netscape browser and was originally called **LiveScript**. Dart has been renamed too—originally, it was called Dash.

Considering the timescale it was written under, JavaScript is a great technical achievement, but in 20 years it has not advanced very much, while web applications have rapidly progressed. Web applications can contain thousands of lines of JavaScript code. Outside of very simple pages, plain JavaScript is not enough anymore, as evidenced by the number of tools and libraries that have sprung up to assist development.

Many of these solutions are created to fix problems with JavaScript, ranging from syntax and features to design and productivity. The language simply was not designed for the type of web application that the modern web requires.

Recent advances in JavaScript engines have produced great leaps forward in performance. The V8 engine that powers the Chrome browser and Node.js has shown great improvement in making new kinds of applications viable. However, the returns from JavaScript virtual machine optimizations have been diminishing over time.

The origins of Dart

Google has a lot of experience with both large web applications and writing web browsers. They clearly have a strong self-interest in a better web platform (so people search more) and an improved developer productivity (to stay ahead of the competition). It is mentioned in Google presentations that a single code change in their Gmail web application takes around 20 minutes to rebuild the site for the developer to test it out.

This harks back to software build times decades ago. The project to fix this problem was started, and Google wanted to share and work with the development community as an open source project.

In 2011, at the GOTO conference, the Dart language and virtual machine was unveiled to the world. Dart is designed to be a "batteries included" project—a complete stack for writing, compiling, testing, documenting, and deploying web applications.

Developed by the Chrome team, the project was founded by Lars Bak (the developer of the Java HotSpot VM and JavaScript V8 Engine) and Kasper Lund (a V8 developer). The aim was both to improve the open web platform by opening up new avenues for high performance client web applications and to improve developer productivity.

The upstart language was designed to have a familiar 'curly brackets' syntax similar to Java, C-sharp, and JavaScript, run on both the client and the server, and to support the full range of modern web browsers by being able to compile to regular JavaScript. New language features were only added to Dart if they could be compiled satisfactorily to JavaScript.

Dart is often referred to as **DartLang** to avoid confusion with other "darts." Keep this in mind when searching the Web for better results. The Dart language, like JavaScript, is not only meant for the web browser; it is also available for server applications and command-line applications. Future targets are mobile applications on iOS and Android.

That is the history, the challenge, and the reaction of the biggest Internet company in the world. So, what is Dart all about, then? The remainder of this chapter will compare and contrast Dart and JavaScript and take you into building your first Dart application so that you can see for yourself.

The rest of this book will take you on a tour of Dart through a set of interesting projects, exploring all of Dart's habitats. We will be building useful applications straight away and using increasingly powerful features.

Downloading the tools

Let's get started by installing a complete Dart development environment on your computer. The home of Dart on the Internet is https://www.dartlang.org, which contains the software, a wealth of documentation, and links to the online Dart community.

I would strongly recommend signing up for the e-mail lists on this site to keep up with Dart, and also the Dartisans Google+ community (http://g.co/dartisans). The number of daily messages can be overwhelming at first, but there are some great discussions and information sharing. It is also a great opportunity to interact with Dart's creators.

> It is recommended that you use the Stable channel. This version updates roughly every few months via a built-in update tool. There is also a **Dev** (**development**) channel that updates once or twice a week with the very latest code from the Dart developers. This is great for seeing new features early, but it is not as polished or reliable as the Stable releases.

The downloads for all supported platforms (Linux, Mac, and Windows) are available at https://www.dartlang.org/tools/download.html. The same location provides information regarding building from source. Ensure that you download both the SDK and Dartium (a specialist browser).

It is recommended that Mac users use the Homebrew system to manage the installation and updates of Dart. Linux users can use a .deb if that format is supported on their distribution, with ZIP archives being the alternative. Windows versions are also supplied as ZIP archives.

Windows users can download, install, and update the SDK and Dartium using the Chocolatey installation system that is built on nuget and Powershell.

 See http://chocolatey.org for more information.

The Dart packages are called dart-sdk and dartium.

Introducing the WebStorm IDE

WebStorm is the premiere development environment for Dart and was created by JetBrains, which also publishes IntelliJ IDEA for Java and ReSharper for .Net.

WebStorm is a commercial package available at https://www.jetbrains.com/. There are free licenses available for many and deep discounts for individuals. It supports a range of languages and development platforms and Dart support is provided via a plug-in. The plugin comes pre-installed with the IDE.

Download the installation file and follow the installation steps on screen:

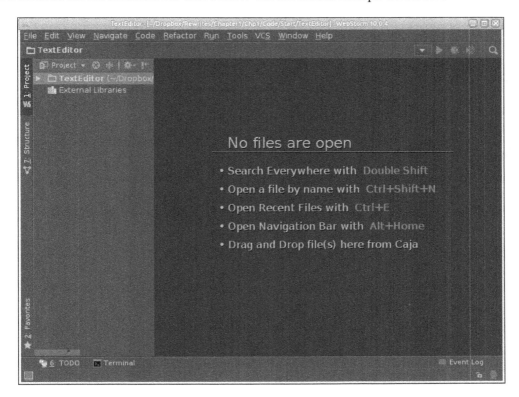

WebStorm has a number of powerful features to help write our web applications:

- Auto-completion of code: properties and methods are listed as you type
- A static analyzer that scans as you type for possible problems
- Refactoring tools to help rename entities and extract methods
- Quick fixes to correct common errors easily
- Navigation via a code tree and finding usages of a function
- A code reformatter to keep the source code in a tidy format
- A powerful debugger

Alternative development environments

If you wish to use another IDE, there are plugins for IntelliJ IDEA and Eclipse. If you prefer a simple text editor, there are plugins for Sublime, Emacs, and Vim. These are all listed on the DartLang download page.

If you are an avid Visual Studio user, there is a community project underway to bring Dart to that environment. DartVS can be downloaded from the Visual Studio Gallery. It directly uses the DartAnalyzer from the SDK to report errors, warnings, and hints inside the IDE. Support for intellisense and other features is underway, too.

The Atom Editor (`https://atom.io/`) is an alternative for those who prefer a lightweight editor to a fully fledged development environment. The plugin, named `dartlang` (`https://atom.io/packages/dartlang`) provides code-completion, syntax highlighting, and access to some `pub` commands.

Help starting a project

To help create your new project, Dart has a tool called Stagehand that creates the scaffolding from a high quality project template of your choice. It takes care of common tasks such as folder structure, common libraries, and style sheets. It even has its own website (`http://stagehand.pub/`).

In WebStorm, creating a new project presents you with a range of powerful options, allowing you to set the locations of the Dart SDK and choose a project type for sample content. The project type gives a range of skeleton applications and is powered by the Stagehand application that is part of the SDK:

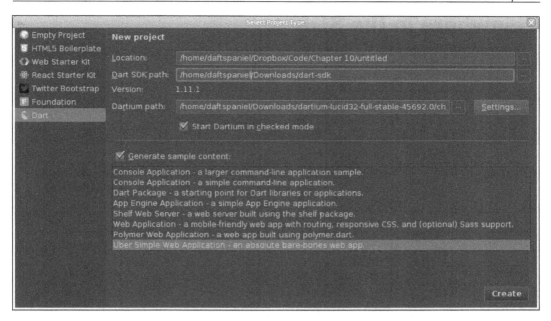

`Stagehand` can also be run from the command line, with the first step being to install it as a command:

```
pub global activate stagehand
```

This step installs the `stagehand` command from the `stagehand` package:

```
mkdir aproject
cd aproject
stagehand web-full
```

This will create a folder of sample content based on the web-full template.

 For full details of the current templates, see

`https://pub.dartlang.org/packages/stagehand.`

Elsewhere in the SDK

The download also includes a set of command-line tools, which can be found under the `dart-sdk/bin` path.

Tool	Description
`dart`	The standalone Dart Virtual Machine itself.
`dart2js`	The tool that converts Dart into JavaScript so that it can run on any modern browser.
`Dartanalyzer`	Analyzes the Dart source code for errors and suggestions. This is also used by development environments to provide feedback to users.
`Dartdocgen`	The documentation generator that works directly on Dart code.
`Dartfmt`	The intelligent code formatter that makes your code tidy and consistent.
`pub`	The package management and application deployment tool.

You may wish to place these tools on the system PATH so that you can call them from anywhere on the command line. This is optional as WebStorm provides an easy interface to these tools; however, many developers find it essential to a good workflow.

For more detailed information on the installation and configuration of pub, see

`https://www.dartlang.org/tools/pub/installing.html`

Also in this location is a snapshots folder. Most of the tools are written in Dart itself; when they are started up and initialized, a binary image of the initialized state can be stored and used for future executions of the program.

The snapshots are generated using the Dart executable and are mostly intended for frequently used command-line applications in deployment.

Building your first application

Starting simple is a good idea, but we also want to start with something useful that can be expanded as we explore Dart.

In day-to-day software development, the text editor is where gigantic, world-changing software often starts. We are going to build a multi-purpose web-based text editor to use as a scratchpad for snippets of code, a to-do list, or stripping formatting from copied text—immensely handy. For added realism, there will be an imaginary customer along the way asking for new features.

In the next chapter, we will build on this foundation for some flashier features and graphical displays.

Downloading the example code

You can download the example code files for all Packt books you have purchased from your account at http://www.packtpub.com. If you purchased this book elsewhere, you can visit http://www.packtpub.com/support and register to have the files e-mailed directly to you.

Exploring the Web project structure

Go to the WebStorm welcome page and click on **Open**. Select the folder where you extracted the sample code and choose the Chapter One folder, then the sub-folder named Start.

A good first step when opening any Dart project is to ensure all dependencies are present and up to date. To achieve this, select pubspec.yaml and right-click to show the context menu. Click on the Pub: Get Dependencies item. The dependencies will then be resolved and fetched if required.

File / Folder	Description
packages	A link to the packages (or libraries) that are being used by this project. In this case, you will see the 'browser' package.
pubspec.lock	Controls the specific version of the packages being used.
pubspec.yaml	Meta information on our project (name, description, and so on) and a list of packages being used.
web/styles/main.css	The standard cascading style sheet file.
web/index.html	The entry point for our web application.
main.dart	Last but not least, a Dart file!

Unwrapping packages

From the preceding list, there is clearly a lot of structure and meta files for packages in even a simple Dart project. The philosophy of the language is that libraries are small, focused, and likely to be from different sources. They are also numerous and update on different schedules, so version controls are important—dependencies are hungry and must be fed.

You want your team members to be able to build and use your new Uber package without dependency horrors! Likewise, you want the package you download off the Internet to "just work" and reduce the effort required to write your application.

To look after all these packages, Dart has a tool called `pub`. This is a Swiss Army knife tool that helps create, manage, and deploy your programs and packages. The main home for Dart packages is the website `https://pub.dartlang.org`, where numerous open source libraries are published.

 If you are curious to know the origin of the name, "pub" is British slang for a bar where people drink and play a game of darts.

A look at Pubspec

The `pubspec.yaml` has a curious file extension — YAML stands for **Yet Another Markup Language:**.

```
name: 'TextEditor'
version: 0.0.1
description: A web based text editor.
environment:
  sdk: '>=1.0.0 <2.0.0'
dependencies:
  browser: any
```

From this, it is clear to see `pubspec.yaml` is Dart's equivalent of a project or solution file. This holds the typical dependency details and meta-information. The `Pubspec` file is fully detailed at `https://www.dartlang.org/tools/pub/pubspec.html`. Although it is an extensive and powerful file, the main interaction you will probably have with it is adding new dependencies.

Putting Dart into the web page

The file `index.html` is a regular web page. The rest of the file consists of a few simple `<div>` elements and, as you might expect, a `<textarea>` tag:

```
<!DOCTYPE html>
<html>
<head>
    <title>TextEditor</title>
    <link rel="stylesheet" href="styles/main.css">
</head>
```

```
<body>
<div id="output">

    <div id="toolbar">
    TextOnTheWeb
    </div>

    <textarea id="editor" cols="80" autofocus>
    </textarea>

</div>
<script type="application/dart" src="main.dart"></script>
<script data-pub-inline src="packages/browser/dart.js"></script>
</body>
</html>
```

The foot of this page is where the initial Dart file is specified. The main.dart file is loaded and the entry point, the first function to be run, is the main() function.

 If you have programmed in C/C++, C#, or Java, main is a familiar starting or entry point to an application. The concept is identical in Dart.

Let's work through the main.dart file section one at a time and discover some Dart features along the way.

Importing packages

Dart features a keyword, import, to use other packages and classes in our current code context. In this case, both are prefixed with dart: to signify they are from the SDK:

```
import 'dart:html';
import 'dart:convert' show JSON;
```

The keyword show modifies the second import to only make the JSON property sections of the dart:convert package. This limits the classes in the current namespace and therefore helps avoid name clashes and developer confusion.

Variable declarations

The TextArea is central to our editor and will be referenced multiple times; therefore, we will use a specific type for it rather than var. In contrast, JavaScript declares variables with the all-encompassing var keyword.

```
TextAreaElement theEditor;
```

This declares a new variable called theEditor and declares it as the type TextAreaElement. The dart:HTML package contains classes to cover the DOM and the TextArea input element.

Dart has an optional type system, so it would be possible to declare var theEditor and the program would still run successfully. By being specific with the type, we gain clarity in the source code and we provide more detailed information to developer tools, such as code editors and documentation generators:

```
void main() {
  theEditor = querySelector("#editor");
  theEditor
      ..onKeyUp.listen(handleKeyPress)
      ..text = loadDocument();
}
```

In the main function, we use the querySelector method from dart:HTML to connect to the TextArea control (with the ID attribute set to editor) on the web page. Once we have a reference to the control, we want to a) connect an event handler so that we know when the user has typed something, and b) load any existing text and display it.

Because we are using the same object, we can use the cascade operator (..), which helps us write very readable and flowing code. The preceding can be written as:

```
theEditor.onKeyUp.listen(handleKeyPress);
theEditor.text = loadDocument();
```

The more properties we set, the more we have theEditor cluttering up the code. With the cascade operator, we can replace the object name with (..), and call the method/set a property as before. One important point with the cascade operator is that only the final use has a semi-colon at the end of the line.

Writing the event handler

The editor's `TextArea` `KeyUp` event has been connected to this short handler function:

```
void handleKeyPress(KeyboardEvent event) {
  saveDocument();
}
```

In contrast to JavaScript, there is no `function` keyword and we have `void` before the function. The `void` keyword just means that this function does not return anything when it is finished; it can be any class or type. As Dart is optionally typed, we could omit `void` altogether.

Just a minute! Where are we going to be storing this text? After all, we have only written a single HTML page and do not have a database connection or web service to take care of the persistence. Fortunately, HTML5 has a simple key/value based built-in storage feature called Local Storage that is well-supported by modern web browsers. This operates in a similar fashion to a dictionary (sometimes called a map) data structure.

In the next two functions, we will look at loading and saving from `localStorage`.

 The HTML5 feature `window.localStorage` persistently stores data with the client's browser. Unlike data stored in cookies, it does not expire based on a date. The data is not lost when the browser window is closed or the computer is switched off.

The amount of storage can vary per browser and according to user settings, but the typical default value is 5 MB. This is plenty for our text editor and many other types of applications.

Loading the saved text

The `loadDocument` function lets the world know it will be returning a `String` object:

```
String loadDocument() {
  String readings = "";
  String jsonString = window.localStorage["MyTextEditor"];
  if (jsonString != null && jsonString.length > 0)
    readings = JSON.decode(jsonString);
  return readings;
}
```

We will store the text under the key `MyTextEditor`. The first time the user loads up this page, there will be nothing in the local storage for our web page, so we will check if it is empty or null before putting the value into the `readings` string variable.

JSON (JavaScript Object Notation) is an ECMA standard data format that is based on a subset of JavaScript and is an alternative to XML.

For example:

```json
{
    "Name": "Davy Mitchell",
    "LuckyNumber": 123,
    "CarModel": null,
    "Language": "English"
}
```

Saving the text

The format we are using to save the text is JSON — JavaScript Object Notation — which is a common standard in web pages. The package `dart:convert` gives us both the encode and decode functions:

```dart
void saveDocument() {
  window.localStorage["MyTextEditor"] = JSON.encode(theEditor.value);
}
```

Finally, the saved document uses the local storage to keep our text safe. This time, we are encoding the data into the JSON format.

Running in the browser

We are now finally ready to actually run the text editor in the target environment. How is a browser going to execute a `.dart` file? Internet Explorer, Chrome, and Firefox don't speak Dart.

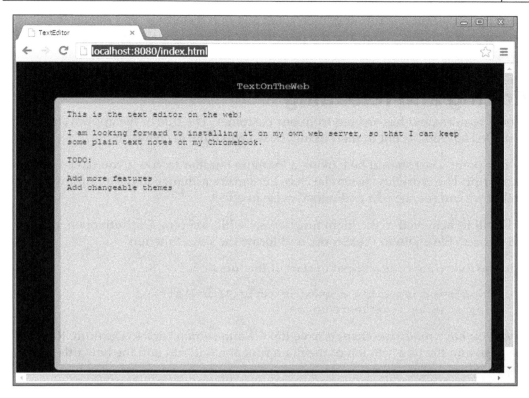

Dartium is a special build of the Chromium browser (the open source project behind Google's Chrome browser) that contains the Dart virtual machine. Though not recommended for day-to-day browsing, it is a full powerful modern browser to use while developing Dart applications. As shown in the screenshot, it looks just like (a very plain) Google Chrome.

> If you are running on Ubuntu and receive a start up error mentioning `libudev.so.0`, run the following command in a terminal to resolve it:
>
> ```
> sudo ln -s /lib/x86_64-linux-gnu/libudev.so.1 /lib/
> x86_64-linux-gnu/libudev.so.0
> ```
>
> For more information, see `https://github.com/dart-lang/sdk/issues/12325`

In WebStorm, right-click on the `index.html` file to bring up the context menu and select the run `index.html`. This will start a local HTTP server for your application.

Once the application is running, type some text into the editor, and then close the browser window. Then, run the program again and you should see your text reappear once the page has loaded.

Editing and reloading

A new requirement has arrived from our customer. The title of the application, "TextOnTheWeb", is not to their liking, so we will have to change it.

By this point, Dart should be looking a lot more familiar to you if you have written JavaScript. The workflow is similar, too. Let's make a change to the executing code so that we can see the edit and reload cycle in effect.

This will be achieved in the main function so, while keeping Dartium open, open the main.dart file again in WebStorm, and locate the main function.

Add the following code snippet to start of the function:

```
DivElement apptitle = querySelector("#toolbar");
apptitle.text = "TextEditor";
```

Once you have made the change, save the file and switch back to Dartium. Refresh the page and the new version of the main function will run and the new title will be displayed.

Extending the interface

Our customer has asked for a button to clear the editing area. This is a reasonable request and should not take too long to code with the productivity of Dart.

Firstly, we will open the index.html and add an input button to the page underneath the TextArea control:

```
<input type="button" id="btnClearText" value="Clear" />
```

Open main.dart and in the main function, connect up an event handler:

```
ButtonInputElement btnClear = querySelector("#btnClearText");
btnClear.onClick.listen(clearEditor);
```

As with JavaScript, it is very easy to pass functions around as parameters. Move the cursor over the text clearEditor and a lightbulb will appear. This offers the keyboard shortcut of *Alt* and the *Enter/Return* key, or you can click on the lightbulb icon.

```
void main() {
    theEditor = querySelector("#editor");
    theEditor
        ..onKeyUp.listen(handleKeyPress)
        ..text = loadDocument();
}
                        Create function 'loadDocument'
```

The implementation of the function is straightforward. Notice that we receive a properly typed `MouseEvent` object as part of the event:

```
void clearEditor(MouseEvent event) {
    theEditor.text = "";
    saveDocument();
}
```

Refresh the page and click the button to clear the existing text. One happy customer and we hardly broke a sweat!

The WebStorm Dart plugin has a number of quick fixes to aid your productivity and help avoid coding errors in the first place. They also encourage good design and keeping to Dart conventions.

Using the CSS editor

Keep the text editor running for the moment and switch back to WebStorm. Go to the **Project** tab and in the `TextEditor` folder, open the `web/styles/main.css` file.

This is going to be your editor, too, so it is important that it is your favorite color—perhaps you would like a thinner border or are not too fond of my chosen gray palette.

Make some changes to the color classes and save the file.

The WebStorm CSS editor is powerful and shows previews of colors. If you switch back to Dartium and click reload, the text editor should now reflect your chromatic preferences.

Debugging a Dart application

A good debugger is a key part of a productive development system. Let's step through our code so that we can look closely at what is going on.

To debug an application running in Dartium from WebStorm, we need to install a small browser extension to act as a bridge between the two applications.

 Follow the guide from JetBrains at the following web page:
`https://www.jetbrains.com/webstorm/help/using-jetbrains-chrome-extension.html`

The main section to be concerned with is the "Installing the JetBrains Chrome extension" section. This only has to be done once.

1. Click on the first line of the `loadDocument` function.

2. Next, open the **Run** menu and choose **Toggle Line Breakpoint**. A red circle will appear to the right of the line:

```
16
17  String loadDocument() {
18     String readings = "";
19     String jsonString = window.localStorage["MyTextEditor"];
20     if (jsonString != null && jsonString.length > 0)
21       readings = JSON.decode(jsonString);
22     return readings;
23  }
24
```

3. Select `index.html` in the **Project** tab, then open the **Run** menu and choose the `Debug index.html` menu.

4. Once Dartium opens, the `loadDocument` function should run and the breakpoint should hit. The **Debugger** tab will appear in WebStorm.

5. The **Debugger** tab shows the call stack and values of current variables. Under the **Run** menu and on the toolbar, the usual debug operations of **Step Into**, **Step Over**, and return are available.

6. Before we take any steps, hover the pointer over the return statement line. A tool-tip will appear to show that the string `variable readings` is currently set to `null`.

7. Choose **Step Over** and the execution will move onto the next line.

8. Move the pointer over the return statement again, and the readings variable is shown to be an empty string object.

9. **Step Over** until the end of the function, and the return variable will be set to the text retrieved from local storage.

10. To get the application running again, use the **Resume Program** menu option from the **Run** menu, or to stop it from running, select the **Terminate** menu option.

Working in harmony with JavaScript

The clear button on the editor is a bit dangerous as it may wipe out some vital notes. We will provide the user with a simple *Are you sure?* prompt so that they have a chance to back out of the operation.

You are probably thinking that we could use the Dart equivalent of `window.confirm` to carry it out. We certainly could, but to demonstrate the ability to call JavaScript, we will use the non-Dart version to display a prompt to the user.

Open `main.dart` and add the following import to the top of the file:

```
import 'dart:js';
```

In the **Dart Analysis** tab directly below the Dart code editor window, you will see a warning that we have an unused import. This can be a useful tip once a project has grown and code has been moved around into separate packages and classes. Import lists can soon acquire clutter.

To call the JavaScript confirm dialog, we use the context object from `dart:js` in the button click event handler. The context object is a reference to JavaScript's global object:

```
void clearEditor(MouseEvent event) {
  var result = context.callMethod('confirm',
      ['Are you sure you want to clear the text?']);
  if (result == true) {
    theEditor.text = "";
    saveDocument();
  }
}
```

The `callMethod` method can be used to call any JavaScript function available in the scope of the page—not just built in objects. In this case, the first parameter is the name of the function we wish to call and the second parameter is the list of arguments for that method.

Commenting in the code

Our text editor foundation is looking complete at this point, but there is one important element that is missing from the `main.dart` file—code comments.

Dart uses the following familiar commenting syntax:

Comment Syntax	Description
// Your comment here.	A single line comment
/** Your comment here. */	A multiple line comment
/// Your comment here.	A doc comment (the preferred method because it is more compact)

In mentioning an identifier, place square brackets around the name. For example:

```
/// Returns double of [a] input.
int doubleANumber(int a){
    //Assumes parameter valid.
    return a * 2;
}
```

Take a short time to comment each function with the above style. Use a sentence format and punctuation.

For more information on comment style and other coding conventions, see the guidelines for Doc comments:

`https://www.dartlang.org/articles/doc-comment-guidelines/`, and the Dart coding style guide: `https://www.dartlang.org/articles/style-guide/`

Summary

This chapter was focused on giving you the background story of Dart and getting to work with the SDK to produce a useful application.

We have discovered how the JavaScript language and its development limits, leading to the creation of the Dart open source project (centered around the `https://www.dartlang.org` website), which is being developed as an ECMA standard and can be used to write a range of application types from client to server and command line.

We have seen that Dart has a familiar syntax and powerful package management tool called `pub`. WebStorm can be used to create, launch, and debug different types of applications, and other IDEs and text editors have Dart language support, too.

We have worked through setting up a Dart development environment and wrote our first application using HTML5 features. We saw how to navigate the structure of a client-side web project and carry out debugging and development.

I am certain that the simple text editor that we have created is firing off ideas in your mind of what to do next! In the next chapter, we will continue to look at client-side Dart and add more features to the text editor, including some that will help us write more, and better, Dart code.

2
Advancing the Editor

We made the buttons on the screen look so good you'll want to lick them.

– Steve Jobs

The technical possibilities of ever shinier web designs and more smoothly animated layouts that modern web browsers are capable of makes the challenge of balancing features and attractive presentation even harder for web application developers.

Functional and non-functional requirements, such as interface design and performance, are often conflicting priorities. There is only a finite amount of time for any project. A good strategy (sometimes!) is to focus on those that deliver both, and there are many new possibilities within the expanding HTML standard.

Once the requirements are all settled and the application is constructed, deploying the applications to the production environment smoothly is key. Testing on our target systems, such as a range of web browsers, is vital, and that is where we are heading with this chapter.

The next steps for the text editor

We have had some feedback on the text editor so far. Users like it and want more buttons, and the top priority is a word-count feature that displays a dialog with the current count. Customers have has indicated that they would like a powerful toolbar above the editor pane for a range of features. They like the pop-up dialog style, but say that the current one does not fit into the look of the application.

Starting point

Open the code sample for *Chapter 2, Advancing the Editor* `texteditor` to see a slightly modified version of the project from the first chapter. It is not ready to run out of the box as we will add in a `package` to deal with the dialog creation.

The text editor functionality has been moved into a separate file—our `main.dart` was getting rather cluttered. My personal preference is to keep it as minimal as possible. The `main.dart` now imports a file, `editor.dart`, and the main function is used to connect the interface to the `Editor` object, which now contains our functions as methods of the `TextEditor` class.

Dart is an object-orientated language like C# and Java. In object-orientated languages, objects can be defined as class declarations that typically group together variables and functions to model an aspect of a system. For more information on object-orientated programming, see `https://en.wikipedia.org/wiki/Object-oriented_programming`.

For example, web browsers have the `document` and `window` classes that can be accessed from JavaScript. These objects encapsulate aspects of the web page structure and web browser window in functions and properties.

Even if you have not written classes with JavaScript, you will likely have called functions and accessed properties on the built-in browser page objects such as the `document.getElementById()` method and the `document.body` property.

Dart classes

We have already encountered classes for HTML elements and event handlers. Dart has an advanced single-inheritance class system. Classes are declared with the `class` keyword. The `editor.dart` file has a class for the `TextEditor` (an abbreviated version is shown below):

```
class TextEditor {
    final TextAreaElement theEditor;
    ...
    TextEditor(this.theEditor){
    ...
    }
    ...
}
```

The constructor is declared as the same name of the class, and we have a single parameter. Dart constructors have a convenient feature for directly setting member variables from the parameter declaration. This saves having a separate parameter that is only ever used to assign to the member variable. Without using this shorthand feature, the code would be as follows:

```
class  TextEditor {
    final TextAreaElement theEditor;
    ...
    TextEditor(TextAreaElement theEditor){
    this.theEditor = theEditor;
    }
    ...
}
```

The field `theEditor` is declared as final; this means it can only be assigned a value once in the lifetime of the application.

Structuring the project

Our new requirements are for two pop-up dialogs, and it sounds like we may need more. We need to build an HTML interface library to cover these needs. It is general-purpose, so can be used in many types of application. The rest of the application can go in the `TextEditor` project.

Building the dialog package

The `pub` packaging system is a great resource for sharing finished packages online. If we want to keep a package local and private, we can create it locally and use it in much the same manner.

The package project structure

The package project is structured in a similar manner to a web application project, with a pubspec.yaml file being the main project file. Instead of a web folder, there is a lib folder containing the simple_dialog.dart file that declares our library and defines what is exposed outside the project:

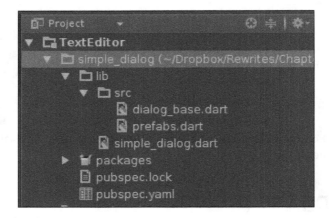

This file contains any classes, functions, and references to other files—in this case, the two files in the src folder. The first line in simple_dialog.dart with the keyword library states the name and declares that this is a library. Note that it is not surrounded by any quotation marks:

```
library simple_dialog;
import 'dart:html';
part 'src/dialog_base.dart';
part 'src/prefabs.dart';
```

The next section contains the imports required for all the files that are being exposed by this package declaration in the part declarations. Open either of the files in the src folder and you will see part of simple_dialog declared on the first line.

Adding a local package reference

To reference the library, go to the `TextEditor` project's `pubspec.yaml` and open it in the editor. Click on the **source** tab to see the plain `yaml` text file. There is currently no graphical interface for the local reference, so it has to be added by hand:

```
dependencies:
browser: any
intl: any
simple_dialog:
path: ..\simple_dialog
```

The path is relative to the root project directory, and, as this is a local filesystem reference, the path separator must match the operating system, so we use \ (backslash) for Windows and / (forward slash) for Linux and Mac.

The package is then referenced in `editor.dart` with a `package` prefix:

```
import 'dart:convert';
import 'dart:html';
import 'package:simple_dialog/simple_dialog.dart';
```

It operates in exactly the same way as a remotely installed package, with the added advantage that it automatically refreshes if changes are made.

> To avoid any problems with relative paths (which make many people's heads hurt!), if possible, keep projects in the same directory so that the relative path is always the same. Alternatively, full paths can be used, although this may introduce problems when the code is on different computers.
>
> To verify that the path is right, look in the `Project` tab, expand the `Packages` folder, and the package should be listed with its source.
>
> Path dependencies are useful for local development, but will not work when sharing projects with the wider world.

Understanding the package scope

Dart operates under a library scoping system. All items in a package are available throughout—there are no private or protected assets at this level. However, items inside the library can be kept private to external code.

To achieve the equivalent of a private field, a field of a class can be marked private if it has a preceding _ (underscore) character. Any project referencing the library can only use the assets that the package has exposed.

For example, the `TextEditor` project can use the `Dialog` class that is public by default and access the `content` field, but not the `_visible` field.

Defining the base dialog box

The dialog core is defined in the `Dialog` class in the `dialog_base.dart` file. This will contain all the foundational functionality, such as the dialog frame and the **OK** and **CANCEL** buttons. More specialized dialog boxes will inherit (`extend`) this class and modify it for their purposes.

The package will contain common dialogs for the following:

- A simple alert dialog box
- An application about dialog box
- Confirmation dialog from the user

The alert dialog box

This is the simplest of all the dialogs. It will show a line of text and allow the user to press the **OK** button so that the dialog box is dismissed:

```
void alert(String dlgTitle, String prompt, int width, int height) {
  Dialog dlg = new Dialog(dlgTitle, prompt, width, height, true,
false);
  dlg.show();
}
```

The dialog box does not return any value, and to make this as easy as possible for the user, it is a single function call. This will be used to display the result of the word-count feature.

The About dialog box

The standard About box for an application contains a small amount of information and a link to a website. This dialog is visually identical to the Alert box apart from the addition of the hyperlink, and as this involves changing the dialog interface elements, this will be implemented in a new class called AboutDialog:

This is created from the showAbout method of the TextEditor object:

```
void showAbout(MouseEvent event) {
  AboutDialog textEditorAbout = new AboutDialog(AppTitle,
  "TextEditor for the Web", "http://www.packtpub.com", "Homepage",
300, 200);
  textEditorAbout.show();
}
```

The AboutDialog box inherits from the Dialog class and calls the constructor of the Dialog class via super, which calls the constructor to form the foundation of the object:

```
AboutDialog(String titleText, String bodyText, this.linkUrl, this.
linkText, int width, int height)
: super(titleText, bodyText, width, height, true, false){
```

The elements for the box are created and added to the nodes member of the content `DivElement`:

```
content..nodes.insert(0, new BRElement())
  ..nodes.insert(0, new BRElement())
  ..append(new BRElement())
  ..append(new BRElement())
  ..append(link)
  ..style.textAlign = "center";
```

The `cascade` operator keeps the code compact and focused on setting up the different components of the dialog.

Using the confirmation dialog box

This dialog presents **OK** and **CANCEL** options, and calls a specified function if the former option is clicked. This is used in the `TextEditor` class `clearEditor` method:

This is implemented by using the base `Dialog` class directly:

```
void confirm(String dlgTitle, String prompt, int w, int h, Function
action) {
  Dialog dlg = new Dialog(dlgTitle, prompt, w, h);
  dlg.show(action);
}
```

The application can configure and display this dialog with a single line:

```
confirm(AppTitle, "Are you sure you want to clear the text?",
400, 120,
performClear);
```

A function is passed to the show method that is performed if the user presses the **OK** button.

Counting words using a list

Word count is an important feature for students, technical writers, and competition entrants. Our customers see this as a required feature, too.

In the event handler, we want to calculate the word count and throw the dialog on screen for the user to see. This is a simple, short-running task, so the implementation can exist directly in the event handler. As the output is simple, the alert dialog can be used.

To determine the word count, Dart's List data structure and String classes can be used. The first step is to remove any punctuation characters that may affect our count. This is declared in custom_dialogs.dart as an unmodifiable const string as it can be used for other word-based features:

```
const String punctuation = ",.-!\"";
```

This is used in the showWordCount method of the TextEditor class.

Once the punctuation is removed, the string can be split into a List. Dart supports generics, so the types of general data structure can be optionally specified, in this case with <String>. The list of words is then filtered to clean out any non-word entries remaining.

Once we have obtained the list of words, the final word count can be obtained by using the length property of the list.

The Word Frequency feature

Our customers would like a feature to help with writing quality. Overuse of particular words can make a text repetitive and hard to read. To determine the frequency of word usage, Dart's `Map` (sometimes called an associative array or dictionary), data structure class, and `String` features can be used:

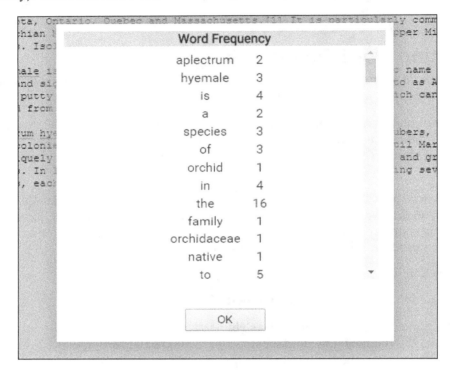

Depending on the number of different words used, the content areas may be allowed to scroll, as the dialog cannot grow to the size of any data.

Generics are used again to specify the types for the key and value; in this case, `String` for the key and `int` for the value:

```
Map<String, int> wordFreqCounts = {};
String out = "";

for (var character in punctuation.split(''))
  text = text.replaceAll(character, " ");
text = text.toLowerCase();
```

```
List<String> words = text.split(" ");
words
  ..removeWhere((word) => word == " ")
  ..removeWhere((word) => word.length == 0)
  ..forEach((word) {
    if (wordFreqCounts.containsKey(word))
      wordFreqCounts[word] = wordFreqCounts[word] + 1;
    else wordFreqCounts[word] = 1;
  });

wordFreqCounts
    .forEach((k, v) => out += ("<tr><td>$k</td><td>$v</td></tr>"));
```

The processing of the text is similar to the word count, where a list of individual words is built up. Once the list is filtered, `forEach` is used to iterate through the list and count the occurrences of each word. The `forEach` method is used again to build the output HTML, with the map's key and value parameters being passed to the function.

Understanding the typing of Dart code

The types used so far for the `Map` and `List` help the design-time tools, such as the Dart Analyzer and WebStorm, which allows us to write code by providing the code completion and validating assignments.

When run in Dartium with the checked mode enabled (the default setting), types are checked at runtime. In the final environment, most likely a web browser such as Firefox or Internet Explorer, the typing information is not used and does not affect the execution speed of the application.

Dart coding recommendations advise using types on all public-facing code. For example, a class in a package can use private `var` variables, but methods require and return typed data. This aids developers calling the code in understanding what is required, and helps create better documentation.

The file download feature

It can be very useful to have an actual file, so we will add a feature to let the user download and save the contents of the editor to their local device. This is possible with the custom data attributes feature in HTML5, which supports text as one of the formats:

```
void downloadFileToClient(String filename, String text) {
  AnchorElement tempLink = document.createElement('a');
  tempLink
    ..attributes['href'] =
    'data:text/plain;charset=utf-8,' + Uri.encodeComponent(text)
    ..attributes['download'] = filename
    ..click();
}
```

The process is straightforward: an anchor element is created and its target is set as the encoded text data. The click event is then fired and the download proceeds as if it were being downloaded from a web server.

The clock feature

Everyone has deadlines, so keeping an eye on the clock is important. The dart:async package can help with this task by using a Timer class to trigger and update. This can be carried out in one line in main.dart file of the TextEditor project:

```
new Timer.periodic(newTimer.periodic(new Duration(seconds: 1),
(timer) => querySelector("#clock").text =
(new DateFormat('HH:mm'))
            .format(new DateTime.now())
                );
```

The Timer constructor being called here (Timer.periodic) is a specially named constructor; in this case, the periodic version is being used. There are numerous variations of Timer objects. Named constructors allow the classes to have instances easily created for a particular purpose as they do not require additional initialization configuration before they are ready to use.

A periodic Timer will fire an event every duration period; in this case, one second. The remainder of the line declares the function that is called. Dart has a shorthand of => for functions that are a single line (which are named arrow functions), thus avoiding the use of curly brackets. The querySelector function is used to get a reference to the element on the web page with an ID of clock where the time will be displayed.

The current time is obtained and formatted into hours and minutes for display. As the clock will run for the lifetime of the application and does not require any interaction, no variable is required to store a reference to the object.

That was a busy line of code, and very powerful, but we are not finished examining it yet! There has been no extra thread or process created. This is not a user-initiated event. We will take a look at the what and when of the Dart task queue.

Executing Dart code

The internal architecture of the Dart VM has a single-threaded execution model that is event-driven. In Dart terminology, this is called an isolate. The execution of a Dart program places each event (for example, a function call) into one of two queues. The VM then takes the next event and executes it.

The first queue is the main event queue, and the second is called the microtask queue. This second queue is a higher priority, but is reserved, as the name implies, for short, small tasks, such as creating a new event or setting a value:

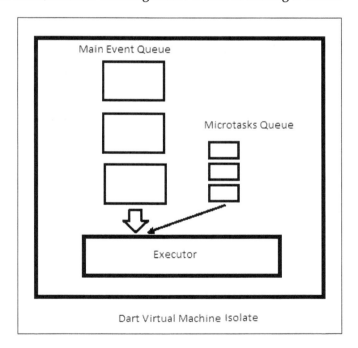

This execution detail is hidden from the Dart developer for the most part. However, it is important to understand that execution of Dart code is highly asynchronous. The aim of this is to allow applications to continue to be responsive, while still performing longer tasks such as calculations or accessing remote resources.

The advantage of such architecture is the complete removal of the need for any locking or synchronization during program execution. Other virtual machines have to do this, and this greatly affects complexity and performance. For example, Python's **GIL (Global Interpreter Lock)** has been debated for years, with many alternatives suggested and experimentally implemented.

Multi-processing the VM

The design of the Dart VM allows multiple isolates to run simultaneously, which can be running across different threads, CPU cores, and, in the web browser, web workers. They do not share any resources such as memory, and their sole form of communication is through a messaging system.

The class designer

The customers want a feature that will appeal to programmers. They would like a way for the user to quickly sketch out ideas for a class, including details such as the class name, fields, and methods.

Building a more complicated dialog

To handle this feature, a custom dialog will be required—GenClassDialog in custom_dialogs.dart. This will inherit (extend) the Dialog class, and handle the **OK** button click event handler itself. Unlike the other dialogs so far in the application, this dialog must return a piece of data back to the text editor:

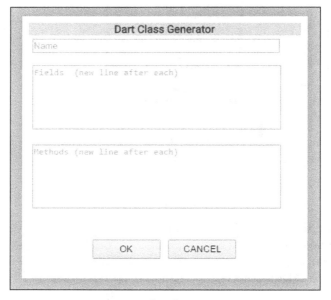

The input controls are one `TextInputElement` and two `TextAreaElements`. The `placeholder` property, available in modern web browsers, will be used to guide the user on what to enter, and, as a bonus, they are convenient space savers, as we do need to add extra elements to label the inputs:

```
String className = name.value;
String fieldsSrc = "";
String methodsSrc = "";

List<String> classFields = fields.value.split("\n");
List<String> classMethods = methods.value.split("\n");

classFields.forEach((field) => fieldsSrc += "    var $field;\n");
classMethods.forEach((method) => methodsSrc += "    $method(){};\n");
```

The text is retrieved from the controls and split by line into lists. The method `forEach` is then used to traverse the list and build the source code.

Constructing the class

The template of a simple class in the `GenClassDialog makeClass` method has placeholders for the generated source code of the fields and methods. This class code template is declared as a multi-line string using three double-quote characters. Dart supports string interpolation, which helps when putting values of variables into strings:

```
result = """   /// The $className Class.
class $className {

$fieldsSrc

    $className(){}

$methodsSrc

    }
    """;
```

Variables can be embedded in strings prefixed by a $ sign. These are then replaced with the actual value of the variable when the string is used.

It is also possible to insert more complicated code, such as an objects property, `"The word is ${text.length} characters long"`. Note the use of curly brackets around the expression being evaluated.

Understanding the flow of events

The dialog for creating the class source code is created and handled by the
`TextEditor` class located in the `editor.dart` source file.

The sequence of events to display the dialog display is as follows:

1. The `showClassGen` event handler constructs the class and puts it on screen, and the function completes, leaving the dialog visible to the user.

2. The user fills in the details and hits the **OK** button. This event triggers the `OK pressed` method on the `ClassGenDialog`.

3. The text is extracted from the fields and the source code in the `ClassGenDialog makeClass` method. Then, the `resultHandler` is called.

4. The `resultHandler` is the `createClassCode` method on the editor that sets the `TextAreaElement` as the constructed source code.

Launching the application

To launch the application and try the text editor application for yourself, select
`index.html` in the **Project** tab, right-click to bring up the context menu, and click on
Run 'index.html'. This `Run` command is also available in the **Run** menu on the main
WebStorm menu bar.

The command-line app for source code statistics

Our customers like the software development angle of the text editor and has asked
for some source code statistics such as **SLOC (source lines of code)** to be made
accessible. This feature may be of use outside the web page, such as in a continuous
integration environment, so we will construct our first command-line application.

We will create the project in WebStorm from scratch, but a completed version is also
supplied in the sample code in a folder called `dart_stats`.

The command-line project structure

Open WebStorm, click on **Create New Project**, and select **Console application** from the **Project Templates** list. Choose a location for your project and call it dart_stats.

The structure of the application has a bin folder with main.dart, which is the entry point for the application. This is where the main function is located. The project template contains several other items. For this tool, the focus will be on the main function.

 Dart is cross-platform, and the majority of filesystems used by the OS platforms are case-sensitive. It is a highly-recommended convention that all filenames are lowercase.

Add the source code file sourcescan.dart to the project. This contains the code for scanning the text and tallying up line counts for classes, code, comments, imports, and whitespace.

Processing the source code

The SourceCodeScanner class contains five integer fields to store the counts and a single method to perform the analysis:

```
void scan: (List<String> lines) {
    totalLines = lines.length;
    lines.forEach((line) {
      line = line.trim();
      if (line.startsWith("class")) classes++;
      else if (line.startsWith("import")) imports++;
      else if (line.startsWith("//")) comments++;
      else if (line.length == 0) whitespace++;
    });
}
```

The list of lines is iterated over and the trim method is used to remove extra whitespace from the lines to aid in matching the keywords that trigger and increment the count. The startsWith method makes sure that the keyword is not appearing mid-line in another context.

File handling with the dart:io package

The application will be passed a single command-line argument, which is the full file path to a Dart source code file. The command-line arguments can be read from the parameter passed to the main function in main.dart.

One aspect that we will not have to deal with in the browser is loading the source code from a text file. A package that is not available to Dart in the web browser, due to security, is the IO package, which contains direct file handling functionality:

```dart
import 'sourcescan.dart';
import 'dart:io';

main(List<String> arguments) {
  print(arguments[0]);
  SourceCodeScanner codeScan = new SourceCodeScanner();
  File myFile = new File(arguments[0]);
  myFile.readAsLines().then((List<String> Lines) {
    codeScan.scan(Lines);
    print("${codeScan.totalLines}");
    print("${codeScan.classes}");
    print("${codeScan.comments}");
    print("${codeScan.imports}");
    print("${codeScan.whitespace}");
  });
}
```

Once the text file is in a string, it can be processed in the same manner as in the web text editor.

The program can be run from the command-line, as shown here on Linux:

```
$ dart bin/main.dart   lib/dartstats.dart
lib/dartstats.dart
9
0
3
0
2
```

The program can examine its own source code!

For more advanced handling of command-line arguments, see the very powerful `args` package on `pub` at `https://pub.dartlang.org/packages/args`.

`readAsLines` is an asynchronous function that immediately returns a `Future` object. A function is passed into the future object's `then` method. The timing of the execution of this function is unknown to the developer. The flow of the program continues straight away. When the file read operation is run and has completed, the function passed to the `then` method is executed when the Dart VM schedules it.

To see this in action, move the print statements outside of the `then` function, as shown, and run the program again:

```
. . .
    myFile.readAsLines().then((List<String> Lines) {
      codeScan.scan(Lines);
    });
    print("${codeScan.totalLines}");
    print("${codeScan.classes}");
    print("${codeScan.comments}");
    print("${codeScan.imports}");
    print("${codeScan.whitespace}");
. . .
```

The probable output is all zeros as the code lines have not been scanned yet; this is because the `print` functions are being called first.

It is also possible that the program will run just as before. The key point is that the overall program execution keeps moving forward even when the code is asked to perform a potentially long-running task, allowing other tasks to continue and keeping the application responsive.

Debugging the command-line program

If you launch the program as it is in WebStorm by using `Run`, then it will open up the debugger with a `RangeError` exception. This is because the program is assuming that a command-line argument has been passed and the program has been run without any input.

In WebStorm, launches of programs into debugging can be configured, including a feature to set command-line arguments. In this case, a full file path to a Dart source file should be put in the **Program arguments** field. Note that, by default, no command-line arguments are passed. It is also possible to set multiple launches with different sets of command-line options:

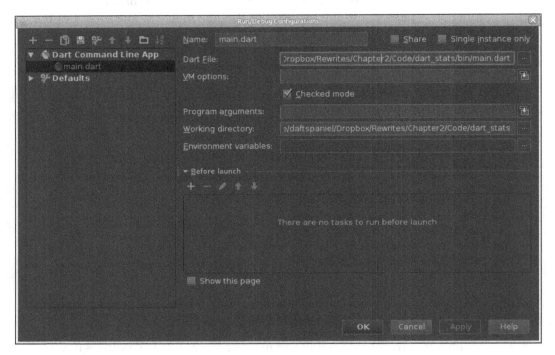

To configure launches, select the **Edit Configurations** option from the **Run** menu. Select `main.dart` from the list and enter the full file path of any Dart source code file, such as one for the sample code for this book or from the Dart SDK.

Once the program is run, the results are printed to standard output using the `print` function.

Integrating the statistics

The class `SourceStats` can be added to the text editor project by adding the `sourcescan.dart` file to the `bin` folder and referencing it as a straightforward import. The scan is to be performed on the contents of the editor in the `scanCode` method of the `CodeStatDialog`, and the data is to be extracted for drawing on the pie chart.

HTML5 and the canvas

Given that the `Canvas` HTML element has been around for approximately 10 years since Apple introduced it into their version of Webkit, it seems odd that it is still considered a new feature! Widespread support has been seen in the major and minor browsers for several years now.

The canvas element provides a high-performance 2D raster-based graphics bitmap that can be scripted dynamically. In contrast to SVG, there are no scene graphs or selectable objects, just a graphic image. It provides an easy-to-use and powerful way to display dynamic images on the client side for applications such as graphs, animations, and games:

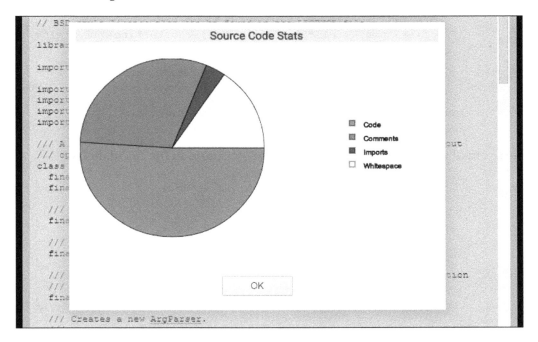

Drawing the pie chart

The four pieces of data collected are to be represented as segments in a pie chart.
In the CodeStatsDialog constructor, the canvas HTML element is selected in the
same manner as any other page element. A **2D** context is requested, which returns an
object we can call methods on to draw on the Canvas:

```
CanvasElement graphs = new CanvasElement();
graphs.width = 500;
graphs.height = 270;
c2d = graphs.getContext("2d");
contentDiv..append(new BRElement())..append(graphs);
```

The stroke is the pen to be used and the fill is analogous to the paint. Each pie
segment is drawn in a black outline (stroke) and painted in with the fill:

```
for (int i = 0; i < 4; i++) {
  c2d
    ..fillStyle = colors[i]
    ..strokeStyle = "black"
    ..beginPath()
    ..moveTo(radius, radius)
    ..arc(radius, radius, radius, lastpos,
        (lastpos + (PI * 2.0 * (data[i] / totalLines))), false)
    ..lineTo(radius, radius)
    ..fill()
    ..stroke()
    ..closePath();
  lastpos += PI * 2.0 * (data[i] / totalLines);
  print(lastpos);
```

The arc method uses radians, so the constant PI is used in the calculations:

```
c2d
  ..beginPath()
  ..strokeStyle = "black"
  ..fillStyle = colors[i]
  ..fillRect(380, 90 + 20 * i, 8, 8)
  ..strokeRect(380, 90 + 20 * i, 8, 8)
  ..strokeText(labels[i], 400, 100 + 20 * i)
  ..stroke()
  ..closePath();
```

The labels are drawn for each of the four counts by using a square `Rect` to show the color, and the text is drawn alongside it.

 The canvas is a versatile feature, but it can be frustrating when nothing appears on it. This often occurs when `beginPath` is used and the path has not been closed with `closePath`.

Building web interfaces with Dart

The `dart:html` package is not the only option for building web interfaces with Dart. The main contenders are Polymer and Angular:

- Polymer (`https://www.polymer-project.org/`) is a JavaScript framework for creating reusable web components (using the Web Component standard) that are encapsulated and inter-operable. They take the form of custom HTML elements. For example, the dialogs in this chapter could be made into web components. To use them in a page, we would use the tags `<DialogConfirm>` and `<DialogWordCount>`, which would avoid a set of nested `div` elements. `Polymer.dart` is the Dart version of the framework and is available from `pub`.

- Angular (`https://angularjs.org/`) is a framework for dynamic data views and is a giant in the JavaScript world. Again, there is a Dart version, called `Angular.dart`. The forthcoming Angular 2 will be written in Typescript and will support both JavaScript and Dart.

Whichever framework or package is chosen, it is likely to use `dart:html` classes at some point, so it is worthwhile to be familiar with them. Not every developer or application needs a framework, so be pragmatic!

Compiling to JavaScript

It is great that we have our enhanced text editor application running in Dartium, but that is not what most web users have installed. What if I want to use it in my daily-driver web browser; for example, Firefox or Internet Explorer?

In order to run on the entire modern Web, Dart code can be compiled via a tool called dart2js (written in Dart) to high quality and performance JavaScript. This can be run as a `pub` command:

```
pub build --mode=release
```

We first encountered this tool when we toured the SDK's command-line tools in the previous chapter. For easy use during development, it is accessible from WebStorm.

In WebStorm's **Project** tab, right-click on the `pubspec.yaml` file, and select **Pub: Build ...**. The **mode** option is then presented for **Release** or **Debug** — for production, choose **Release**. This creates a folder called `build` with the JavaScript version of the program. This can be served by any web server and used from any modern browser:

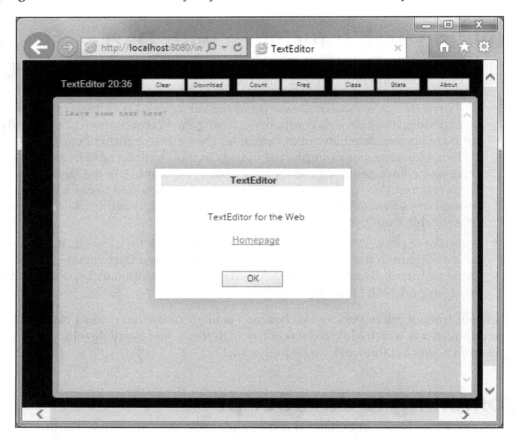

It may be surprising, if text was entered in the Dartium version, that the editor is blank when run from a regular browser. One downside of using local storage is that each web browser has its own independent storage and the user will have to re-enter data if they switch browsers, even if they are on the same computer.

Minification of JavaScript output

The output files from the dart2js compiler can get quite large if certain advanced Dart features are at play, such as mirrors, which are used for reflection (sometimes called introspection).

Fortunately, the default setting of the Dart editor is to produce a minified output. There is always the overhead of the Dart runtime in the JavaScript that is disproportionately large for small applications. As Dart has all the source code ahead of runtime and knowledge of the entire application, it can compile all the code (including packages), determine which are not required, and then, within the packages that are used, remove any parts that are not used.

This sophisticated technique is called tree shaking. Any unused code is shaken off and not included in the final application that is delivered to the end user, keeping it quick to load and execute. Compare this with JavaScript, where if a library is referenced, then the entire library is sent to the client for interpretation.

Summary

The text editor application now has many more useful features, and can be used for a variety of purposes. You are probably thinking of more customized little features you could add to it to help with day-to-day computing. Our imaginary customer has left at this point, so you are in charge now! I am not sure that the buttons are ones I would want to lick, but I would definitely click them for useful functionality.

We have developed a reusable library for creating dialogs that fit in with our application. Dart's data structures, generics, and string handling, are covered from a variety of angles.

We have also achieved an effective presentation of the data through visualizations on the HTML5 canvas, used asynchronous features, and looked deep into the internals of the Dart virtual machine. Finally, we took the application out of the controlled development environment and prepared it for use in any browser by using dart2js.

Text is very powerful, but a little static and hard to read from across a large meeting room. The next step in our Dart journey is to look at animation, presentation, and making some noise.

3
Slideshow Presentations

It usually takes me more than three weeks to prepare a good impromptu speech.

– Mark Twain

Presentations make some people shudder with fear, yet they are an undeniably useful tool for information sharing when used properly. The content has to be great, and some visual flourish can make it stand out from the crowd.

Too many slides can make the most receptive audience yawn, so having the presenter focus on the content and automatically take care of the visuals (saving the creator from fiddling with different animations and font sizes) can help improve presentations. Compelling content still requires the human touch.

Building a presentation application

Web browsers are already a type of multimedia presentation application, so it is feasible to write a quality presentation program as we explore more of the Dart language. Hopefully, it will help us pitch another Dart application to our next customer.

Building on our first application, we will use a text-based editor for creating the presentation content. I was very surprised at how much faster a text-based editor is for producing a presentation, and also more enjoyable. I hope that you also experience such a productivity boost!

Laying out the application

The application will have two modes, editing and presentation. In the editing mode, the screen will be split into two panes. The top pane will display the slides and the lower will contain the editor and other interface elements.

This chapter will focus on the core creation side of the presentation, and the following chapter will focus on the presentation mode and advancing the interface. The application will be a single Dart project.

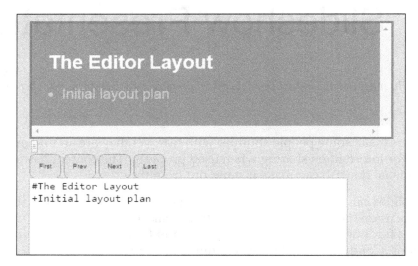

Defining the presentation format

The presentations will be written in a tiny subset of the Markdown format, which is a powerful yet simple to read text file-based format (much easier to read, type, and understand than HTML).

In 2004, John Gruber and the late Aaron Swartz created the Markdown language with the goal of enabling people to write using an easy-to-read, easy-to-write plain text format.

It is used on major websites such as GitHub.com and StackOverflow.com. Being plain text, Markdown files can be kept and compared in version control.

For more details and background on Markdown, see https://en.wikipedia.org/wiki/Markdown

A simple titled slide with bullet points would be defined as:

```
#Dart Language
+Created By Google
+Modern language with a familiar syntax
+Structured Web Applications
+It is Awesomely productive!
```

I am positive you only had to read that once! This will translate into the following HTML:

```
<h1>Dart Language</h1>
<li>Created By Google</li>s
<li>Modern language with a familiar syntax</li>
<li>Structured Web Applications</li>
<li>It is Awesomely productive!</li>
```

Markdown is very easy and fast to parse, which probably explains its growing popularity on the Web. It can be transformed into many other formats.

Parsing the presentation

The content of the `TextAreaHtml` element is split into a list of individual lines, and processed in a similar manner to some of the features in the text editor application using `forEach` to iterate over the list. Any lines that are blank once any whitespace has been removed via the trim method are ignored:

```
#A New Slide Title
+The first bullet point
+The second bullet point

#The Second Slide Title
+More bullet points
!http://localhost/img/logo.png
#Final Slide
+Any questions?
```

For each line starting with a # symbol, a new slide object is created.

For each line starting with a + symbol, they are added to this slide's bullet point list.

For each line discovered using a ! symbol, the slide's image is set (a limit of one per slide).

This continues until the end of the presentation source is reached.

A sample presentation

To get a new user going quickly, there will be an example presentation that can be used as a demonstration and to test the various areas of the application. I chose the last topic that came up around the family dinner table — the coconut as shown in the following code snippet:

```
#Coconut
+Member of Arecaceae family.
+A drupe - not a nut.
+Part of daily diets.
#Tree
+Fibrous root system.
+Mostly surface level.
+A few deep roots for stability.
#Yield
+75 fruits on fertile land
+30 typically
+Fibre has traditional uses
#Finally
!coconut.png
#Any Questions?
```

Presenter project structures

The project is a standard Dart web application with `index.html` as the entry point. The application is kicked off by `main.dart`, which is linked to in `index.html`, and the application functionality is stored in the `lib` folder.

Source File	Description
`sampleshows.dart`	The text for the slideshow application
`lifecyclemixin.dart`	The class for the `mixin`
`slideshow.dart`	Data structures for storing the presentation
`slideshowapp.dart`	The application object

Launching the application

The main function has a very short implementation:

```
void main() {
  new SlideShowApp();
}
```

Note that the new class instance does not need to be stored in a variable and that the object does not disappear after that line is executed. As we will see later, the object will attach itself to events and streams, keeping the object alive for the lifetime that the page is loaded.

Building bullet point slides

The presentation is built up using two classes—`Slide` and `SlideShow`. The `Slide` object creates the `DivElement` used to display the content, and the `SlideShow` contains a list of `Slide` objects.

The `SlideShow` object is updated as the text source is updated. It also keeps track of which slide is currently being displayed in the preview pane.

 Once the number of Dart files grows in a project, the DartAnalyzer will recommend naming the library. It is good habit to name every `.dart` file in a regular project with its own library name.

The `slideshow.dart` file has the keyword `library` and a name next to it. In Dart, every file is a library, whether it is explicitly declared or not.

 If you are looking at Dart code online, you may stumble across projects with imports that look a bit strange, for example:

```
#import("dart:html");
```

This is the old syntax for Dart's import mechanism. If you see this, it is a sign that other aspects of the code may be out of date, too.

If you are writing an application in a single project, source files can be arranged in a folder structure appropriate for the project, though keeping the relative's paths manageable is advised. Creating too many folders probably means that it is time to create a package!

Accessing private fields

In Dart, as discussed when we covered packages, the privacy is at the library level, but it is still possible to have private fields in a class even though Dart does not have the keywords public, protected, and private. A simple return of a private field's value can be performed with a one-line function:

```
String getFirstName() => _name;
```

To retrieve this value, a function call is required, for example, `Person.getFirstName()`; however, it may be preferable to have a property syntax such as `Person.firstName`. Having private fields and retaining the property syntax in this manner is possible using the `get` and `set` keywords.

Using true getters and setters

The syntax of Dart also supports `get` and `set` via keywords:

```
int get score  => score + bonus;
set score(int increase)  => score += increase * level;
```

Using either `get`/`set` or simple fields is down to preference. It is perfectly possible to start with simple fields and scale up to getters and setters if more validation or processing is required.

The advantage of the `get` and `set` keywords in a library is that the intended interface for consumers of the package is very clear. Further, it clarifies which methods may change the state of the object and which merely report current values.

Mixin' it up

In object-oriented languages, it is useful to build on one class to create a more specialized related class. For example, in the text editor, the base dialog class was extended to create an alert and confirm pop ups. What if we want to share some functionality but do not want inheritance occurring between the classes?

Aggregation can solve this problem to some extent:

```
class A {
  classb usefulObject;
}
```

The downside is that this requires a longer reference to use:

```
new A().usefulObject.handyMethod();
```

This problem has been solved in Dart (and other languages) by having a `mixin` class do this job, allowing the sharing of functionality without forced inheritance or clunky aggregation.

In Dart, a `mixin` must meet the following requirements:

1. No constructors can be in the class declaration.
2. The base class of the `mixin` must be the Object.
3. No calls to a super class are made.

`mixins` are really just classes that are malleable enough to fit into the class hierarchy at any point. A use case for a `mixin` may be serialization fields and methods that could be required on several classes in an application and that are not part of any inheritance chain.

```
abstract class Serialisation {
  void save() {
  //Implementation here.
  }
  void load(String filename) {
  //Implementation here.
  }
}
```

The `with` keyword is used to declare that a class is using a `mixin`:

```
class ImageRecord extends Record with Serialisation
```

If the class does not have an explicit base class, it is required to specify an `Object`:

```
class StorageReports extends Object with Serialization
```

In Dart, everything is an object, even basic types such as num are objects and not primitive types. The classes `int` and `double` are subtypes of num. This is important to know as other languages have different behaviors. Let's consider a real example of this:

```
main() {
int i;
print("$i");
}
```

In a language such as Java, the expected output would be **0;** however, the output in Dart is **null**. If a value is expected from a variable, it is always good practice to initialize it!

For the classes `Slide` and `SlideShow`, we will use a `mixin` from the source file `lifecyclemixin.dart` to record a creation and an editing timestamp:

```
abstract class LifecycleTracker {
  DateTime _created;
  DateTime _edited;
  recordCreateTimestamp() => _created = new DateTime.now();
  updateEditTimestamp() => _edited = new DateTime.now();
  DateTime get created => _created;
  DateTime get lastEdited => _edited;
}
```

To use the `mixin`, the `recordCreateTimestamp` method can be called from the constructor and the `updateEditTimestamp` from the main edit method. For slides, it makes sense just to record the creation. For the `SlideShow` class, both the creation and update will be tracked.

Defining the core classes

The `SlideShow` class is largely a container object for a list of `Slide` objects and uses the mixin `LifecycleTracker`:

```
class SlideShow extends Object with LifecycleTracker {
  List<Slide> _slides;
  List<Slide> get slides => _slides;
  ...
```

The `Slide` class stores the string for the title and a list of strings for the bullet points. The URL for any image is also stored as a string:

```
class Slide extends Object with LifecycleTracker {
  String titleText = "";
  List<String> bulletPoints;
  String imageUrl = "";
  ...
```

A simple constructor takes the `titleText` as a parameter and initializes the `bulletPoints` list.

If you want to focus on just the code when in WebStorm, double-click on the filename title of the tab to expand the source code to the entire window. Double-click again to return to the original layout.

For even more focus on the code, go to the **View** menu and click on **Enter Distraction Free Mode**.

Transforming data into HTML

To add the `Slide` object instance into an HTML document, the strings need to be converted into instances of HTML elements to be added to the **DOM (Document Object Model)**. The `getSlideContents()` method constructs and returns the entire slide as a single object:

```
DivElement getSlideContents() {
  DivElement slide = new DivElement();
  DivElement title = new DivElement();
  DivElement bullets = new DivElement();

  title.appendHtml("<h1>$titleText</h1>");
  slide.append(title);

  if (imageUrl.length > 0) {
    slide.appendHtml("<img src=\"$imageUrl\" /><br/>");
  }

  bulletPoints.forEach((bp) {
    if (bp.trim().length > 0) {
      bullets.appendHtml("<li>$bp</li>");
    }
  });

  slide.append(bullets);

  return slide;
}
```

The `Div` elements are constructed as objects (instances of `DivElement`), while the content is added as literal HTML statements. The method `appendHtml` is used for this particular task as it renders HTML tags in the text. The regular method `appendText` puts the entire literal text string (including plain unformatted text of the HTML tags) into the element.

So, what exactly is the difference? The method appendHtml evaluates the supplied HTML and adds the resultant object node to the nodes of the parent element, which is rendered in the browser as usual. The method appendText is useful, for example, to prevent user-supplied content affecting the format of the page and preventing malicious code being injected into a web page.

Editing the presentation

When the source is updated, the presentation is updated via the onKeyUp event. This was used in the text editor project to trigger a save to local storage.

This is carried out in the build method of the SlideShow class, and follows the pattern we discussed in parsing the presentation:

```
build(String src) {
  updateEditTimestamp();
  _slides = new List<Slide>();
  Slide nextSlide;

  src.split("\n").forEach((String line) {
    if (line.trim().length > 0) {

      // Title - also marks start of the next slide.
      if (line.startsWith("#")) {
        nextSlide = new Slide(line.substring(1));
        _slides.add(nextSlide);
      }
      if (nextSlide != null) {
        if (line.startsWith("+")) {
          nextSlide.bulletPoints.add(line.substring(1));
        } else if (line.startsWith("!")) {
          nextSlide.imageUrl = line.substring(1);
        }
      }
    }
  });
}
```

As an alternative to the startsWith method, the square bracket [] operator could be used for line [0] to retrieve the first character. The startsWith method can also take a regular expression or a string to match, as well as a starting index. Refer to the dart:core documentation for more information. For the purposes of parsing the presentation, the startsWith method is more readable.

Displaying the current slide

The slide is displayed via the showSlide method in slideShowApp.dart.
To preview the current slide, the current index, which is stored in the field
currentSlideIndex, is used to retrieve the desired slide object and the Div
rendering method is called:

```
showSlide(int slideNumber) {
  if (currentSlideShow.slides.length == 0) return;

  slideScreen.style.visibility = "hidden";
  slideScreen
..nodes.clear()

..nodes.add(currentSlideShow.slides[slideNumber].getSlideContents
  ());

  rangeSlidePos.value = slideNumber.toString();
  slideScreen.style.visibility = "visible";
}
```

The slideScreen is a DivElement that is then updated off screen by setting the
visibility style property to hidden. The existing content of the DivElement is emptied
out by calling nodes.clear() and the slide content is added with nodes.add. The
range slider position is set, and finally, the DivElement is set to visible again.

Navigating the presentation

A button set with the familiar first, previous, next, and last slide allows the user to
jump around the preview of the presentation. This is carried out by having an index
built into the list of slides and stored in the field slide in the SlideShowApp class.

Handling the button key presses

The navigation buttons require being set up in an identical pattern in the constructor
of the SlideShowApp object. First, get an object reference using id, which is the id
attribute of the element, and then attach a handler to the click event. Rather than
repeat this code, a simple function can handle the process:

```
setButton(String id, Function clickHandler) {
  ButtonInputElement btn = querySelector(id);
  btn.onClick.listen(clickHandler);
}
```

Because `Function` is a type in Dart, functions can be passed around easily as a parameter. Let us take a look at the button that takes us to the first slide:

```
setButton("#btnFirst", startSlideShow);

void startSlideShow(MouseEvent event) {
  showFirstSlide();
}

void showFirstSlide() {
  showSlide(0);
}
```

The event handlers do not directly change the slide; these are carried out by other methods that may be triggered by other inputs such as the keyboard.

Using the Function type

The `SlideShowApp` constructor makes use of this feature:

```
Function qs = querySelector;
var controls = qs("#controls");
```

I find the `querySelector` method a little long to type (though it is descriptive of what it does). With `Function` being comprised of types, we can easily create a shorthand version.

The constructor spends much of its time selecting and assigning the HTML elements to member fields of the class. One of the advantages of this approach is that the DOM of the page is queried only once, and the reference is stored and reused. This is good for performance of the application as, once the application is running, querying the DOM may take much longer.

Staying within the bounds

Using the `min` and `max` functions from the `dart:math` package, the index can be kept in the range of the current list:

```
void showLastSlide() {
  currentSlideIndex = max(0, currentSlideShow.slides.length - 1);
  showSlide(currentSlideIndex);
}
void showNextSlide() {
```

```
    currentSlideIndex =
    min(currentSlideShow.slides.length - 1, ++currentSlideIndex);
    showSlide(currentSlideIndex);
  }
```

These convenient functions can save a great deal of `if` and `else if` comparisons and help make the code a good degree more readable.

Using the slider control

The slider control is another new control in the HTML5 standard. This will allow the user to scroll though the slides in the presentation.

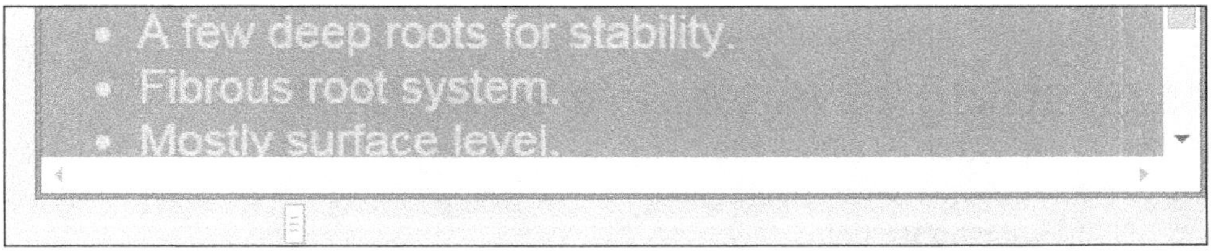

This control is a personal favorite of mine as it is so visual and can be used to give very interactive feedback to the user. It seemed to be a huge omission from the original form controls in the early generation of web browsers. Even with clear, widely accepted features, HTML specifications can take a long time to clear committees and make it into everyday browsers!

```
<input type="range" id="rngSlides" value="0"/>
```

The control has an `onChange` event that is given a listener in the `SlideShowApp` constructor:

```
rangeSlidepos.onChange.listen(moveToSlide);rangeSlidepos.onChange
.listen(moveToSlide);
```

The control provides its data via a simple string value, which can be converted to an integer via the `int.parse` method to be used as an index in the presentation's slide list:

```
  void moveToSlide(Event event) {
    currentSlideIndex = int.parse(rangeSlidePos.value);
    showSlide(currentSlideIndex);
  }
```

The slider control must be kept in synchronization with any other change in its slide display, use of navigation, or change in number of slides. For example, the user may use the slider to reach the general area of the presentation, and then adjust with the Previous and Next buttons:

```
void updateRangeControl() {
  rangeSlidepos
  ..min = "0"
  ..max = (currentSlideShow.slides.length - 1).toString();
}
```

This method is called when the number of slides is changed, and as with working with most HTML elements, the values to be set need to be converted to strings.

Responding to keyboard events

Using the keyboard, particularly the arrow (cursor) keys, is a natural way to look through the slides in a presentation, even in the preview mode. This is carried out in the SlideShowApp constructor.

> In Dart web applications, the dart:html package allows direct access to the globalwindow object from any class or function.

The Textarea used to input the presentation source will also respond to the arrow keys, so there will need to be a check to see if it is currently being used. The property activeElement on the document will give a reference to the control with focus. This reference can be compared to the Textarea, which is stored in the presEditor field, so a decision can be made on whether to act on the keypress or not.

Key	Event Code	Action
Left arrow	37	Go back a slide
Up arrow	38	Go to first slide
Right arrow	39	Go to next slide
Down arrow	40	Go to last slide

Keyboard events, like other events, can be listened to by using a stream event listener. The `listener` function is an anonymous function (the definition omits a name) that takes the `KeyboardEvent` as its only parameter:

```
window.onKeyUp.listen((KeyboardEvent e) {
  if (presEditor != document.activeElement){
  if (e.keyCode == 39)
  showNextSlide();
  else if (e.keyCode == 37)
  showPrevSlide();
  else if (e.keyCode == 38)
  showFirstSlide();
  else if (e.keyCode == 40)
  showLastSlide();
  }
});
```

 It is a reasonable question to ask how to get the keyboard key codes required to write the switching code. One good tool is the W3C's **Key and Character Codes** page at http://www.w3.org/2002/09/tests/keys.html. Although this documentation is helpful with this question, it can often be faster to write the handler and print out the event that is passed in.

Showing the key help

Rather than testing the user's memory, there will be a handy reference to the keyboard shortcuts.

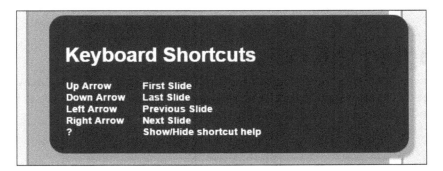

This is a simple `Div` element that is shown and then hidden when the key (remember to press *Shift*, too!) is pressed again by toggling the visibility style from visible to hidden.

Listening twice to event streams

The event system in Dart is implemented as a stream. One of the advantages of this is that an event can easily have more than one entity listening to the class.

This is useful, for example, in a web application where some keyboard presses are valid in one context but not in another. The listen method is an add operation (accumulative) so that the key press for help can be implemented separately. This allows a modular approach, which helps reuse, as the handlers can be specialized and added as required:

```
window.onKeyUp.listen((KeyboardEvent e) {
  print(e);

  //Check the editor does not have focus.
  if (presEditor != document.activeElement) {
    DivElement helpBox = qs("#helpKeyboardShortcuts");
    if (e.keyCode == 191) {
      if (helpBox.style.visibility == "visible") {
        helpBox.style.visibility = "hidden";
      } else {
        helpBox.style.visibility = "visible";
      }
    }
  }
});
```

In a game, for example, a common set of event handling may apply to the title and introduction screen, and the actual in-game screen can contain additional event handling as a superset. This can be implemented by adding and removing handlers to the relevant event stream.

Changing the colors

HTML5 provides browsers with a full-featured color picker (typically, browsers use the native OS's color chooser). This will be used to allow the user to set the background color of the editor application itself:

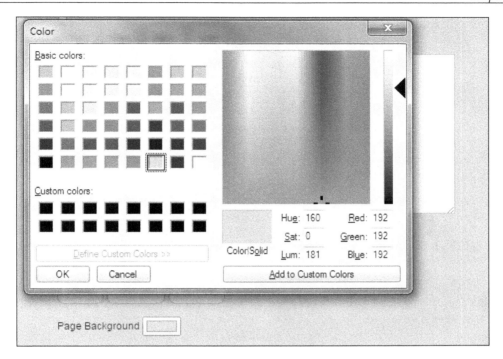

The color picker is added to the `index.html` page with the following HTML:

```
<input id="pckBackColor" type="color">
```

The implementation is straightforward as the color picker control provides:

```
InputElement cp = qs("#pckBackColor");
cp.onChange.listen(
(e) => document.body.style.backgroundColor = cp.value);
```

Because the event and property (`onChange` and `value`) are common to the input controls, the basic `InputElement` class can be used.

Adding a date

Most presentations are usually dated, or at least some of the jokes are! We will add a convenient button for the user to add a date to the presentation using the HTML5 input type date, which provides a graphical date picker:

```
<input type="date" id="selDate" value="2000-01-01"/>
```

The default value is set in the `index.html` page as follows:

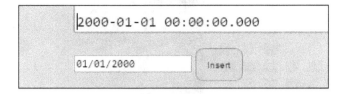

The `valueAsDate` property of the `DateInputElement` class provides the `Date` object, which can be added to the text area:

```
void insertDate(Event event) {
  DateInputElement datePicker = querySelector("#selDate");
  if (datePicker.valueAsDate != null) presEditor.value =
  presEditor.value +
  datePicker.valueAsDate.toLocal().toString();
}
```

In this case, the `toLocal` method is used to obtain a string formatted to the month, day, and year format.

Timing the presentation

The presenter will want to keep to their allotted time slot. We will include a timer in the editor to aid in rehearsal.

Introducing the Stopwatch class

The `Stopwatch` class (from `dart:core`) provides much of the functionality needed for this feature, as shown in this small command-line application:

```
main() {
  Stopwatch sw = new Stopwatch();
  sw.start();
  print(sw.elapsed);
  sw.stop();
  print(sw.elapsed);
}
```

The `elapsed` property can be checked at any time to give the current duration. This is a very useful class as, for example, it can be used to compare different functions to see which is the fastest.

Implementing the presentation timer

The clock will be stopped and started with a single button handled by the `toggleTimer` method. A recurring timer will update the duration text on the screen, as follows:

If the timer is running, the update `Timer` and the `Stopwatch` in the field `slidesTime` is stopped. No update to the display is required as the user will need to see the final time:

```
void toggleTimer(Event event) {
  if (slidesTime.isRunning) {
    slidesTime.stop();
    updateTimer.cancel();
  } else {
    updateTimer = new Timer.periodic(new Duration(seconds: 1),
    (timer) {
      String seconds = (slidesTime.elapsed.inSeconds %
      60).toString();
      seconds = seconds.padLeft(2, "0");
      timerDisplay.text =
      "${slidesTime.elapsed.inMinutes}:$seconds";
    });

    slidesTime
    ..reset()
    ..start();
  }
}
```

The `Stopwatch` class provides properties for retrieving the elapsed time in minutes and seconds. To format this to minutes and seconds, the seconds portion is determined with the modular division operator `%` and padded with the string function `padLeft`.

Dart's string interpolation feature is used to build the final string, and as the elapsed and `inMinutes` properties are being accessed, the `{}` brackets are required so that the single value is returned.

An overview of slides

This provides the user with a visual overview of the slides, as shown in the following screenshot:

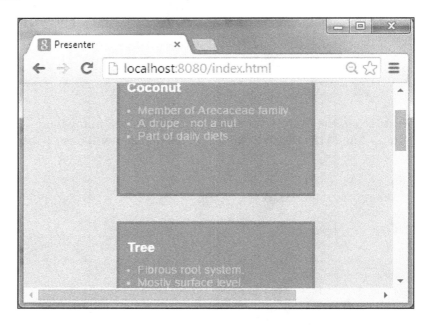

The presentation slides will be recreated in a new full screen `Div` element. This is styled using the `fullScreen` class in the CSS stylesheet located in the `SlideShowApp` constructor:

```
overviewScreen = new DivElement();
overviewScreen.classes.toggle("fullScreen");
overviewScreen.onClick.listen((e) => overviewScreen.remove());
```

The HTML for the slides will be identical. To shrink the slides, the list of slides is iterated over, the HTML element object is obtained, and the CSS class for the slide is set:

```
currentSlideShow.slides.forEach((s) {
  aSlide = s.getSlideContents();
  aSlide.classes.toggle("slideOverview");
  aSlide.classes.toggle("shrink");
  ...
```

The CSS `hover` class is set to scale the slide when the mouse enters so a slide can be focused on for review. The classes are set with the `toggle` method, which either adds if not present or removes if they are. This method has an optional parameter:

```
aSlide.classes.toggle('className', condition);
```

The second parameter, named `shouldAdd`, is *true* if the class is always to be added and *false* if the class is always to be removed.

Handout notes

There is nothing like a tangible handout to give presentation attendees. This can be achieved with a variation of the overview display:

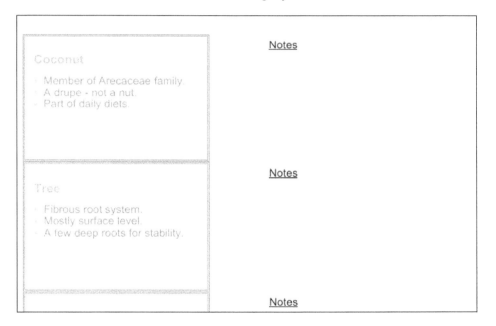

Instead of duplicating the overview code, the function can be parameterized with an optional parameter in the method declaration. This is declared with square brackets `[]` around the declaration and a default value that is used if no parameter is specified:

```
void buildOverview([bool addNotes = false])
```

This is called by the presentation overview display without requiring any parameters:

```
buildOverview();
```

This is called by the handouts display without requiring any parameters:

```
buildOverview(true);
```

If this parameter is set, an additional `Div` element is added for the `Notes` area and the CSS is adjusted for the benefit of the print layout.

Comparing optional positional and named parameters

The `addNotes` parameter is declared as an optional positional parameter, so an optional value can be specified without naming the parameter. The first parameter is matched to the supplied value.

To give more flexibility, Dart allows optional parameters to be named. Consider two functions—the first will take named optional parameters and the second will take positional optional parameters:

```
getRecords1(String query,{int limit: 25, int timeOut: 30}) {
}

getRecords2(String query,[int limit = 80, int timeOut = 99]) {
}
```

The first function can be called in more ways:

```
getRecords1("");
getRecords1("", limit:50, timeOut:40);
getRecords1("", timeOut:40, limit:65);
getRecords1("", limit:50);
getRecords1("", timeOut:40);

getRecords2("");
getRecords2("", 90);
getRecords2("", 90, 50);
```

With named optional parameters, the order they are supplied in is not important and has the advantage that the calling code is clearer as to the use that will be made of the parameters being passed.

With positional optional parameters, we can omit the later parameters, but it works in a strict left-to-right order, so to set the `timeOut` parameter to a non-default value, the limit must also be supplied. It is also easier to confuse which parameter is for which particular purpose.

Summary

The presentation editor is looking rather powerful with a range of advanced HTML controls, moving far beyond text boxes, date pickers, and color selectors. The preview and overview help the presenter to visualize the entire presentation as they work, thanks to the strong class structure built using Dart `mixins` and data structures using generics.

We have spent time looking at the object basis of Dart, how to pass parameters in different ways, and, closer to the end user, how to handle keyboard input. This will assist in the creation of many different types of applications, and we have seen how optional parameters and true properties can help document code for ourselves and other developers.

Hopefully, you learned a little about coconuts, too!

The next step for this application is to improve the output with full screen display, animation, and a little sound to capture the audience's attention. The presentation editor could be improved, as well—currently, it is only in the English language. Dart's internationalization features can help with this.

4

Language, Motion, and Sound

The sound and music are 50% of the entertainment in a movie.

– George Lucas

A slideshow presenter would be a poor choice of application to create a movie, but even with a smaller audience, there are lessons to be learned from those who have mastered the silver screen.

Simple animations in user interfaces are pleasing to the eye and enhance the overall experience.

Sounds have been present in web browsers for some time now, largely depending on plugins. Most users will be glad that the days of the autoplaying MIDI file are long gone, and most developers will be pleased that there will finally be a standard way to play sound files.

Going fullscreen

A slide show has been in the small screen mode so far and needs to be moved to a web browser equivalent of **IMAX**—fullscreen mode. The audience doesn't want to see a slideshow editor or desktop—just the slides.

 To open the sample code project of this chapter, open the `Presenter` folder in WebStorm and then open the `slideshowapp.dart` file.

Request fullscreen

While the trend in web browsers has been to gradually reduce the size of screen controls—a trend accelerated by the Chrome browser—fullscreen web applications are still being accepted by users and standards are settled between the browsers. Lets have a look at the following screenshot:

For security, the web browser will prompt the user to give permission for the website to enter the fullscreen mode, which hides toolbars and status bars that are offscreen.

Once the fullscreen mode is entered, the user is notified of the domain that takes over the entire screen. The web browser also sets the Escape (*Esc*) key as a means for the user to exit the fullscreen mode. After a few seconds, it floats off the screen and can be brought back by moving the pointer back to the top of the screen.

The exact behavior and positioning may vary according to your web browser and operating system. For example, Internet Explorer tends to display notifications at the bottom of the page.

The requestFullscreen method is available on most page elements, though typically, div will be used as a container. The presenter application calls the setupFullScreen method from the constructor of the SlideShowApp object. A Boolean flag is used to keep track of the display mode:

```
qs("#btnStartShow").onClick.listen((e) {
    isFullScreen = true;
    liveFullScreen
      ..requestFullscreen()
      ..focus()
      ..classes.toggle("fullScreenShow")
      ..style.visibility = "visible";
```

```
      liveSlideID = 0;
      updateLiveSlide();
    });
```

The onFullscreenChange event can be listened to so that an individual element can listen to the change in state. For example, a toolbar may not appear when the application is in fullscreen mode.

When you click on div, the isFullScreen flag is set, fullscreen is requested, and the input focus is set on the liveFullScreen object. Next, the .css file is set on div and it is made visible on screen. Finally, liveSlideID is set at the start of the presentation and the display is updated with the slide's contents.

Updating the interface for fullscreen

The editor screen will need a button to start the slideshow in fullscreen mode. The display will be an entirely new element and not just an enlarged editor preview.

Fullscreen will be a div element that fills the entire window and contains child div elements for background, complete with a background image, and the slide that is currently being displayed.

Updating keyboard controls for fullscreen

An event listener similar to the one implemented for the editor screen in the previous chapter is required here. The keyboard controls are set up in the setupKeyboardNavigation method of the SlideShowApp class:

```
void setupKeyboardNavigation() {
  //Keyboard navigation.
  window.onKeyUp.listen((KeyboardEvent e) {
    if (isFullScreen) {
      if (e.keyCode == 39) {
        liveSlideID++;
        updateLiveSlide();
      } else if (e.keyCode == 37) {
        liveSlideID--;
        updateLiveSlide();
      }
    } else {
      //Check the editor does not have focus.
      if (presEditor != document.activeElement) {
        if (e.keyCode == 39) showNextSlide();
        else if (e.keyCode == 37) showPrevSlide();
```

```
        else if (e.keyCode == 38) showFirstSlide();
        else if (e.keyCode == 40) showLastSlide();
    }
  }
});
```

The isFullScreen flag is used to determine which mode the presentation application is in. When in the fullscreen mode, liveSlideID is incremented or decremented depending on the key pressed and the currently updated displayed slide.

Adding mouse controls

Clicking on the mouse button to advance the presentation is a fairly common feature and our application should support this too. This is implemented in the setupFullScreen method:

```
liveFullScreen = qs("#presentationSlideshow");
liveFullScreen.onClick.listen((e) {
  liveSlideID++;
  updateLiveSlide();
});
```

The onClick event is listened to on the fullscreen div element, and the slideshow is advanced to the next slide when this request is received. Let's have a look at the following screenshot:

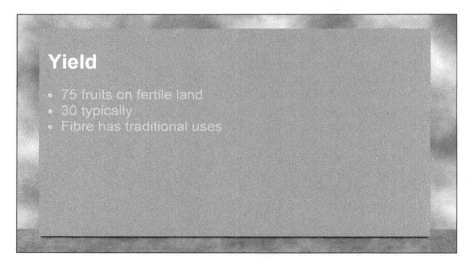

Adding metadata

At the time of writing, some of the fullscreen APIs are marked as experimental in the Dart API documentation, and this is made clear in the documentation as well. By the time you read this, the fullscreen APIs should hopefully be stabilized and fully operational.

This is the normal process for new web browser features, which are eventually made stable. The adding of experimental APIs is likely to be a continuous process — it seems very unlikely that web browsers will ever be 100 percent complete! The `onFullscreenChange` Dart API documentation reads:

```
Experimental
ElementStream<Event> get onFullscreenChange
Stream of fullscreenchange events handled by this Element.
```

The source code for this part of the `dart:html` package has several annotations including the `@experimental` marker:

```
/// Stream of `fullscreenchange` events handled by this [Element].
@DomName('Element.onwebkitfullscreenchange')
@DocsEditable()
// https://dvcs.w3.org/hg/fullscreen/raw-file/tip/Overview.html
@Experimental()
ElementStream<Event> get onFullscreenChange =>
fullscreenChangeEvent.forElement(this);
```

Dart has a very flexible annotation system, and new systems can be created to add metadata to most of the components in Dart, such as classes, functions, and libraries. The pattern, as you probably already spotted, is used to start them with a @ sign followed by a call to the `const` constructor or a reference to a compile-time constant variable.

Creating a custom annotation

Let's create our own `Temporary` annotation that will mark classes as temporary to the design of the application and will allow a label to record which planned build the temporary classes are scheduled to be removed:

```
import 'dart:mirrors';

class Temporary {
  final String removalBuildLabel;
  const Temporary(this.removalBuildLabel);
```

```
    String toString() => removalBuildLabel;
}

@Temporary('Build1')
class TempWidgetTxt {}

@Temporary('Build2')
class TempWidgetWithGFX {}

void main() {
  ClassMirror classMirror1 = reflectClass(TempWidgetTxt);
  ClassMirror classMirror2 = reflectClass(TempWidgetWithGFX);

  List<InstanceMirror> metadata1 = classMirror1.metadata;
  print(metadata1.first.reflectee);

  List<InstanceMirror> metadata2 = classMirror2.metadata;
  print(metadata2.first.reflectee);
}
```

The `Temporary` constructor allows a label to be set. This field must be `final` (a single-assignment variable or field) if this class is to be used as an annotation. The main function calls `reflectClass` to obtain the details of the classes and then accesses this metadata and stores it in a list. The `toString` method allows the metadata to be the output via `print`:

```
Build1
Build2
```

Annotations are used extensively in the core Dart APIs, and in packages, they are used as the basis of frameworks, for example, web applications. They are not an obscure feature of the core SDK.

Translating the user interface text

My first ever professional software release did not involve any creation of code. It was a language update release for an existing package, and it was just as satisfying to mail out the CD-ROM (this was a while ago!) as something I had coded from scratch. Thankfully, it made me famous in Norway!

The translation of a software application is critical for its acceptance in some markets. This is even more true in the world of web applications. Dart has a package called `intl` that is used to help bring your applications to a global audience.

The `presenter` interface needs to be updated so that it displays the editor in French and Spanish. This will involve extracting the strings that we wish to use, obtaining translations, and integrating them back into the project.

The language will be selectable at runtime by user selection. The current OS interface language may not be the language that the user wishes to use the application in.

Exploring the intl package

The `intl` package provides functionality for internationalization and localization of Dart applications. This not only includes the important aspect of translating interface text into other languages but also includes the formatting of text (not every language is formatted from left to right), dates and numbers.

Locating strings to translate

The interface of an application largely consists of buttons, with a few other labels and controls. A phrasebook of the application's interface language can be created using `Intl.message` and stored as static functions in the `PhraseBook` class, which can be found in the `interfacetrans.dart` file. This organizes all the strings that are to be set on the interface elements at runtime using the `value` or `text` properties:

```
class PhraseBook {
  // Navigation controls.
  static String btnFirstSlide() => Intl.message("First",
      name: "btnFirstSlide", desc: "Button label - go to the first
slide.");

  static String btnPrevSlide() => Intl.message("Prev",
      name: "btnPrevSlide", desc: "Button label - go to the previous
slide.");
  ...
```

The functions are static so no instance of the class is required to call the function, so, for example, `PhraseBook.btnFirstSlide()` will return the string for the first slide. `Intl.message` has a series of named parameters. The `name` parameter needs to match the function name for the string extraction tools, which are covered in the next section. The `desc` (description) field provides context of where the string is used on the program. This is useful when the translator does not have access to the software that may not even be written yet.

`Intl.message` has extensive features, such as modifying a phrase due to it being plural or referring to a different gender. Plus, it can store more meta information such as example usages of the string to give the translator more context. Refer to the SDK documentation for more details.

Extracting the strings

The English strings for the application are now organized in a class file. Next, we need to extract the strings so that they can be sent out for translation. The `intl` package contains an extraction tool that can be run from the command line.

 The next section of this chapter deals with the task of running tools from the command line. Ensure that the Dart SDK `bin` folder is on the executable path for your system so that `pub` and other Dart tools can be executed from anywhere on the command line.

Running commands with Dart pub

`Pub` is a tool with many uses in Dart, and one interesting feature of it is to run command-line tools that are part of Dart packages:

```
pub run packagename:programname
```

When this command is issued, `pub` will look for `programname.dart` in the `packages bin` folder:

```
pub run intl:extract_to_arb --output-dir=c:\transarb web\lib\
interfacetrans.dart
```

 Refer to https://www.dartlang.org/tools/pub/package-layout.html for more information on the package structure.

Ensure that the target directory already exists. The final parameter is the source file containing the functions with the translation strings.

The **Application Resource Bundle** (**ARB**) is a JSON-based format that is extensible and directly usable by applications.

You can find out more about the format of the project at `https://code.google.com/p/arb/`.

The JSON format ARB files contain much of the information from the `Phrasebook` class translated into a dictionary declaration:

```
{
"btnFirstSlide":"First",
 "@btnFirstSlide":
     {"description":"Button label - go to the first slide.",
      "type":"text",
...
```

This easy-to-read and portable file format can be used by a range of applications to produce usable translations.

Obtaining translations

Google Translator Toolkit (`https://translate.google.com/toolkit/`) is a powerful online tool that accepts `.arb` files, among other formats. This is free to use and requires a Google account to login.

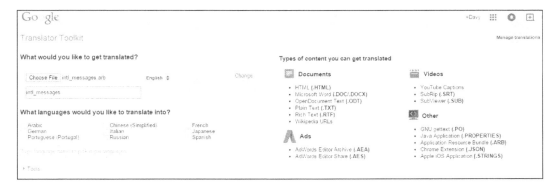

One useful feature of Toolkit is that it is tied to Google Translate so that a computer translation of the text is made available. This is the method that is used for the presentation string resources—it does not give perfect translations but is useful for initial testing and the layout of the interface.

Managing translations for even a small project can be a sizeable amount of work. Every new button means new strings, new translations, and more testing!

One alternative to Google Translator Tooklit is the open source project Pootle, which can be found at `http://pootle.translatehouse.org/`.

From my experience I can tell you that translators come from a range of backgrounds, are not always technically minded, and you have to deal with significant time differences. Time to use those important people-focused soft skills!

Each language can be translated separately and the tool allows progress to be tracked of the translation process. The translation file can be shared with other users and translations can be crowd-sourced if desired.

Once the translation is complete for the language, they can be downloaded as `.arb` files. Let's have a look at the following screenshot:

Integrating the translations text

Now that the translations are safely stored as strings, it is time to bring them back into the Dart project by transforming theses files into Dart source code files.

Notice the naming of the ARB files with _es and _fr that allow the intl:generate_from_arb tool to determine which language is in play. In this case, the Dart files are being put directly into the project in the lib folder:

```
pub run intl:generate_from_arb
--output-dir=web/lib
web/lib/interfacetrans.dart
web/lang/messages_es.arb web/lang/messages_fr.arb
```

The files created include the central messages_all.dart message, which is the main import Dart file. There is also a supporting file created for each language that is being used, messages_es.dart and messages_es.dart.

Changing the language of the user interface

To make use of the translations, the messages_all.dart file needs to be imported into interfacetrans.dart. The intl package needs to be told which language we want to use, and behind the scenes, it deals with loading the correct resources. The setInterfaceLang function in interfacetrans.dart carries out this task and is called by the SlideShowApp constructor:

```
setInterfaceLang(String langID){
  initializeMessages(langID).then((_) {
    Intl.defaultLocale = langID;
    addInterfaceText();
  });
}
```

Best of all, the addInterfaceText method does not need to change, no matter how many new languages are added.

Adding a language combo box

For users and developers, it is useful to change the language of the interface anytime. We will add a combo box with a handler for the onChange event to allow the user to select a language from the list:

```
<select id="interfaceLang">
 <option>en</option>
 <option>fr</option>
 <option>es</option>
</select>
```

All the initialization for the interface has been wrapped in the setInterfaceLang method, so the only parameter that is to be passed is the value from the combo box (SelectElement):

```
setInterfaceLang("en");
qs("#interfaceLang").onChange.listen((e) {
  var lang = qs("#interfaceLang").value;
  setInterfaceLang(lang);
  langInterface = lang;
  . . .
```

This is set up with the other listeners in the SlideShowApp constructor and triggers the change of the interface requested by the user. The language can be switched to a French user interface with a single click at runtime, and the change occurs almost instantly.

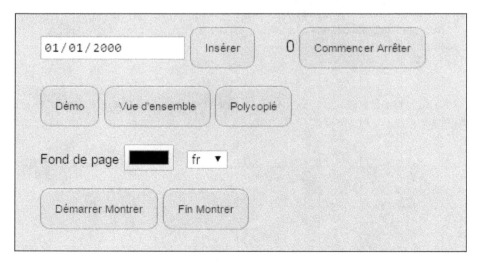

The length of strings can vary wildly from language to language - the button layout allows expansion. Note the differences in button between the Spanish and French translations.

This is a factor to consider when planning the interface layout of your multilingual applications. It is probably best to assume that other languages will be longer and allow some room for expansion.

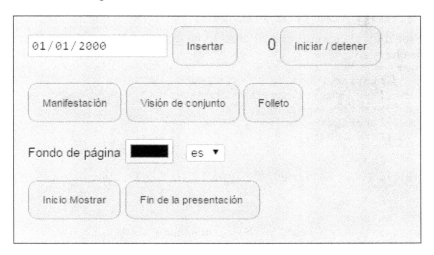

Advanced as the application is, I am afraid that it is left to the user to translate the demo coconut presentation material!

Working with dates

The ISO 8601 standard for dates is 'Year Month Day', and naturally, no country in the world uses this standard day to day! A typical variation is to have the month or day first, and then the separator character is used between digits in shorthand.

The `intl` package can help provide the appropriate format and translations for each language. Translation strings are required too as the name of the day or month may be required.

Date handling is implemented in the `SlideShowApp` class:

```
import 'package:intl/date_symbol_data_local.dart';
```

A field is used to keep a reference to the active `DateFormat` object:

```
DateFormat slideDateFormatter;
```

We will consider how this formatter is initialized and kept up to date with the changes made to the users language.

Formatting for the locale

The locale for the date formatter will need to be updated whenever the interface language is changed:

```
qs("#interfaceLang").onChange.listen((e){
  var lang = qs("#interfaceLang").value;
  setInterfaceLang(lang);
  langInterface = lang;
  initDefaultDate();
});
```

When a locale has been requested, the appropriate `DateFormat` object needs to be created:

```
initDefaultDate() {
  initializeDateFormatting(langInterface, null).then((d) {
    slideDateFormatter = new DateFormat.yMMMMEEEEd(langInterface);
  });
}
```

Once this is in place, it is possible to change the interface language using the combo box and get a date in the correct format and language.

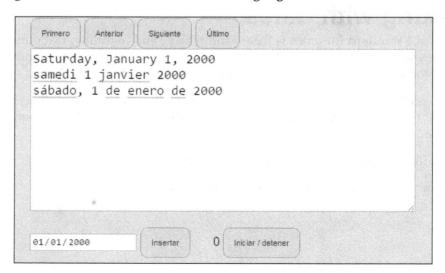

As a final thought on this topic, most web applications are not nearly as dynamic in their choice of language. Typically, an interface language selection is a per user configuration option that is set up for each session when the user logs in.

Animating slides

The fullscreen display only has one slide at any time. A *new* slide will be initially placed on the top of the screen and will be gently lowered into view. The *old* slide will, from the presentation viewer's point of view, vanish instantly.

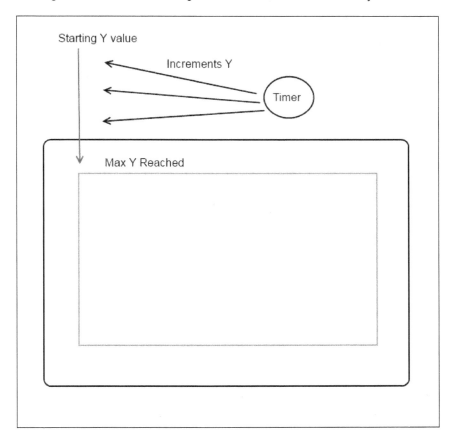

Using a timer

The periodic timer in Dart should be a familiar friend of yours by now. This is used to check whether the slide has reached the final position. If it is not there yet, then the position is updated:

```
new Timer.periodic(new Duration(milliseconds: 50), (timer) {
  if (isFullScreen && liveSlideY < 0) {
    liveSlide.style.top = liveSlideY.toString() + "px";
    liveSlideY += 50;
  }
});
```

You may be concerned that the `Timer` object runs all the time, even when a presentation is not running fullscreen. In reality, they are very lightweight and the work that the animation performs is so minimal that it will have a negligible impact.

Playing sound in the browser

This feature was deliberately left until last as continually listening to the same sound effect can become quite irritating! MP3 is probably the best supported format for various web browsers, with one exception—**Dartium**.

Dartium is built from the Chromium open source project. The project does not include any proprietary codecs including MP3. When creating projects, it is sometimes fine to just use MP3 and test the audio parts of the application in another browser.

For this project, three formats of the same sound file are provided. The OGG format will run from Dartium and most browsers. If you are having trouble, try another format.

Producing sound effects

To create a sound effect to play when the slide changes, a tool such as Bfxr can be used. It can be found on the Web at `http://www.bfxr.net/` (where there are links to downloads for standalone versions as well) and is a powerful audio creation tool.

As it was created for use during game jams (time-constrained game coding contests), it is easy to pick up and fast to use. Let's have a look at the following screenshot:

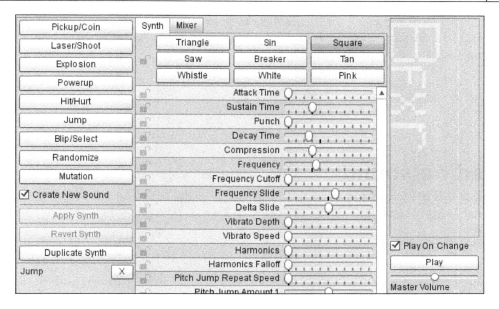

Creating sound files

Audacity (http://web.audacityteam.org/) is a popular and stable audio editing and recording package. It is an open source desktop application and is available for all the major OS platforms. Let's have a look at the following screenshot:

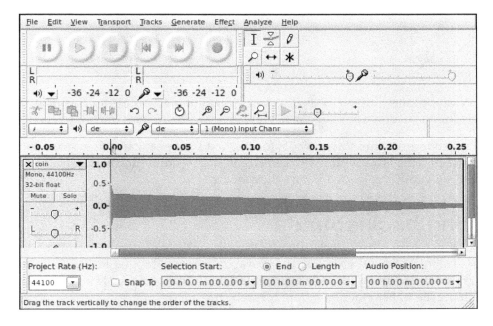

You can perform some last minute tweaks to your sound and export it (**File** | **Export..**) in a variety of formats (such as, MP3, Ogg, and WAV). On some systems, you may need to download an MP3 codec.

 Keep an eye on the file size and duration time, though! Ideally, the sound should be around 200ms long.

Loading sounds

The sound is loaded in a method that is called from the constructor of the `SlideShowApp` object, and as you expect with Dart, this in an asynchronous operation:

```
List loadAudio() {
  slideChange = new AudioElement("snd/slidechange.ogg");
  slideChange.preload = "auto";
  return [slideChange.onLoad.first];
}

playSnd() {
  slideChange
    ..play()
    ..onEnded.listen(done);
}

done(e) {
  slideChange.load();
}
```

The `onLoad` property of `AudioElement` is a stream of load events for this object (it is possible for audio and other media elements to load more than one file).

The first property of this stream waits for the first load event and then stops listening to the stream. This is a useful way to ensure that all media, such as images and sounds for a game, are loaded before they are used.

Playing back sounds

Once all that set up is done, actually playing the audio is merely a case of calling the `playSnd` method and ensuring that the speakers are plugged in! The `onEnded` event is listened to and a callback is provided. This deals with a browser quirk that requires the file to be reloaded before it can be replayed.

That quirk serves to remind us that although audio support in browsers has greatly improved, it is geared toward large media playback, and playing short sound effects can be a little more work than it should be.

Here's a website that you can use to help contribute to Dart development with either bugs or feature suggestions:

`http://dartbug.com`

This redirects (at time of writing) you to a Google Code project. The Google Code service is being wound down but will be kept going for some time for the Chromium project. As the Dart team is part of the Chrome team at Google, it is possible that parts of the project will live on both Google Code and GitHub.

If you have an idea or think you have found a bug, it is a good idea to search the existing issues or discuss it on **Google+** (`http://g.co/dartisans`) or a mailing list before raising that issue.

Summary

The presentation application now has enough features for the final slideshow to be pleasing to the eyes and ears of the receiving audience.

Behind the scenes, the interface can be used by those who speak languages other than English. Also, the software is ready for easy translation into more languages with minimal code changes.

We looked at the powerful metadata features of Dart and saw how they are used in the SDK and user applications. We saw how the `pub` tool allows us to use tools that are in Dart packages.

With the text editor and presenter applications, the client-side story of Dart has been well explored; taking it to the server-side will give us a view of Dart in another habitat!

5
A Blog Server

Forget about someone's resume or how they present themselves at a party. Can they blog or not? The blog doesn't lie.

– Nick Denton

I wish I could remember which was the first blog that I read on the Web, but I do remember reading (and having) diary sections on a home page, long before the term "blog" was invented! Despite the meteoric rise of various social media platforms, blogging has maintained its place.

It is time for us to explore the server side of the Dart story, and a blog gives us great opportunity to explore different aspects of this language. On the server side, new capabilities are made available, as the context is outside the web browser.

The Hello World server example

It is very simple to create a minimal Hello World server in Dart. Open the sample HelloWorld file of this chapter in the Dart editor. This project is a command-line project, so the main.dart file is placed in the bin folder:

```
import 'dart:io';
void main() {
  HttpServer.bind('127.0.0.1', 8080).then(
    (server) {
    server.listen((HttpRequest request) {
      request.response
        ..write('Hello Dart World')
        ..close();
    });
  });
}
```

The output is shown in the following screenshot:

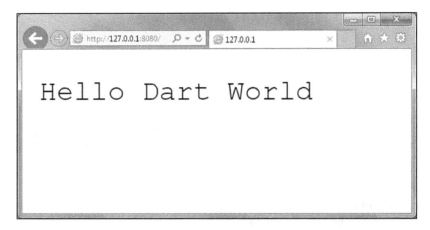

The `dart:io` package is important for the server side. It allows us access to features that are not available to the code running in the web browser context due to security, such as filesystem and networking.

Launching the server program does not open up a web browser like in our previous application. You have to manually open a browser, then go to the address and to the port that you have bound to. Also, if a change is made in the server code, the application has to be stopped and restarted for the change to be seen

The `HttpServer.bind` method takes two parameters—an IP address and a port number. The server is then attempted to be bounded to this network configuration, and if this is successful (and it usually only fails if the binding is already in use), the function is then executed.

Network setups vary from computer to computer. The sample code of this chapter uses ports and IP numbers that are generally available; however, you may have to adjust these for your system—this is likely if you have a busy development system!

The returned server object is set to listen to HTTP requests on that port. If any are received, the message `Hello Dart World` is passed to the `response` method of the `request` object, and then, very importantly, the response is closed.

This simple example shows the structure of all HTTP-based server applications—bind to the network and then handle requests. Of course, handling requests and producing quality output is usually a good deal more complicated.

If you are not too familiar with networking, here is a quick recap! **IP** (**Internet Protocol**) addresses help us identify machines (usually) on the network, and consist of 4 numbers that are separated by a full stop for example 192.168.0.1.

Most computers have a special IP of 127.0.0.1 only for network communications on that machine. This is a computer's network address that is used to create a connection with itself and cannot be used by remote machines. Other than this distinction, it operates as an equal to any other IP address.

Ports help identify which application or service the connection is attached to. For an analogy, IPs are people's names and ports are the topics of conversation. To get the right information, you want to get both correct!

While the application is still running, go to main.dart and change the message, that is the output, by adding ! to the end of the line. Refresh the browser page and you will find that nothing has changed. The Dart code runs on the server and does not get executed in the browser anymore, so the simple refresh feature to see changes is sadly gone now.

The good news is that starting and stopping a server application is very easy, and we can use any web browser to test the application. Breakpoints can still be placed in the code and will be triggered when the page is served.

A blog server

A blog server needs to respond in the same manner to network requests as any other web server so that it can be used by the existing clients. The main clients to the server will be web browsers, such as Google Chrome and Internet Explorer.

A blog server needs to run as a reliable application on different operating systems. Later in this chapter, we will take a look at how a Dart application can be deployed — helper applications and dependencies are required to achieve this.

Introducing the HTTP protocol

The HTTP protocol is straightforward and lightweight. Generally, a server responds to a request with a set of headers stating that the request was successful or not. It then sends the details of what it is going to send, and the content itself, before closing the connection.

The HTTP protocol requires that all headers must be sent before any content. Dart helps enforce this, and if you try to modify the headers once some content has been sent, HttpException will be thrown.

Starting up the server

The `main.dart` entry point for a blog server is similar to the `Hello World` example. The actual functionality of serving the content is handled by the `BlogServerApp` class, of which a single instance is initialized:

```dart
import 'dart:io';
import 'package:blogserver/blogserver.dart';

main() {
  print("starting");
  var blogServer = new BlogServerApp();
  print("Starting blog server...");

  HttpServer.bind('127.0.0.1', 8080).then((server) {
    server.listen(blogServer.handleRequest);
  });
}
```

It is good practice to give some feedback to the user when the server has started. This server is single-threaded, with all requests being handled by one process in a serial manner.

Storing the blog posts format

Blog posts are held in a simple text file format, with the filename being the blog post ID and a `txt` file extension:

```
1st Line - Date
2nd Line - Title
3rd Line until end of file - Post Body
```

A blog post in `1.txt` will look as follows:

```
01/05/2015
Giraffe Facts
<p>
Lorem ipsum dolor sit amet, consectetur adipiscing elit, sed do
eiusmod tempor incididunt ut labore et dolore magna aliqua. Ut
enim ad minim veniam, quis nostrud exercitation ullamco laboris
nisi ut aliquip ex ea commodo consequat. Duis aute irure dolor in
reprehenderit in voluptate velit esse cillum dolore eu fugiat nulla
pariatur. Excepteur sint occaecat cupidatat non proident, sunt in
culpa qui officia deserunt mollit anim id est laborum.
</p>
```

The content is the standard text `Lorem ipsum`, which has been used by typesetters for centuries.

Reading text files

Now that we are working outside the browser, it is possible to work with the file system more directly. Let's take a look at how to read in a text file, and print out each line to the standard output:

```
void main() {
  File myfile = new File("readme.txt");
  myfile.readAsLines().then(
      (List<String> lines)
      {lines.forEach( (line) => print(line) ); }
      );
}
```

To read in a blog post in our defined format, the list of lines needs a little more processing. This is implemented in the process method that is called from the BlogPost constructor in the blog.dart source file:

```
BlogPost(String filename, this._id) {
  File postFile = new File(filename);
  _source = postFile.readAsLinesSync();
  process();
}
```

The file is read using the synchronous version of readAsLines, so the process call does not need to be placed in a then handler, unlike the previous example:

```
process() {

  _html = "";
  _date = _source[0];
  _title = _source[1];

  _html = "<h2>$_title</h2><b>$_date</b><br/>";
  _html += "<img src=\"$_id.png\" align=\"left\">";
  _source.sublist(2).forEach((line) => _html += line);
  _html += "<br/><a href=\"post$_id.html\">Permalink</a>";
}
```

The first two lines are selected using the [] method. The remaining lines are broken off from the list into a sublist, and are directly used to build up the HTML file that will be the output. The content is assumed to be a valid HTML.

Reading a folder of files

In the project, the `posts` subfolder of the `content` folder contains all the blog content. To obtain a list of all the files to load, the `Directory` object can be used to obtain the list, which can be processed with `forEach`:

```
void _loadPostList() {
  Directory blogContent = new Directory(_pathPosts);
  blogContent.list().forEach((File f) {
    String postFilename =
    path.basename(f.path).replaceAll(".txt", "");
    int id = int.parse(postFilename);
    IDs.add(id);
    postPaths[id] = f.path;
  }).then((v) {
    IDs.sort();
    IDs = IDs.reversed.toList();
  });
}
```

The file paths to the blog posts are stored in `Map`, so that they can be retrieved by the `id` value. `IDs` are stored in a list that can then be ordered (there is no guarantee that the filesystem will supply the list of filenames in any particular order), and so that we can easily retrieve posts with the most recently published post first.

Request handling

The incoming `HttpRequest` object contains a wealth of information about the client—the request made and the network connection to the server:

```
handleRequest(HttpRequest request) {

  if (request.uri.path.endsWith(".html")) {
    _serveTextFile(request);

  } else if (request.uri.path.endsWith(".png")) {
    _servePngFile(request);

  } else if (request.uri.path == "/robots.txt") {
    _serveRobotsFile(request);
  }
  else {
    _serve404(request);
  }
}
```

In the context of a blog server, we are most interested in the **Uri** (**Uniform resource identifier**) property, more commonly called a URL, of the `request` object that gives the path of the resource that is requested.

For example, if the request sent to the server is `http://127.0.0.1:8080/post6.html?test=false` (the query string is not used by the blog server), the value of `request.uri` would be `/post6.html?test=false` and `request.uri.path` would have the value `/post6.html`.

For the page, image, or file that is being requested, the `request.uri.path` property gives the desired details. The requests for the `robots.txt` file are handled differently than blog posts and images, and this will be detailed in a later section.

Serving text

If a page is requested, we need to provide feedback to the client making the request. Our response should be firstly to tell the client what format of data we will be responding with (the content type), also known as a MIME type. Secondly, we want to let the client know that we have understood the request (`HttpStatus.OK`), and are about to sent the requested content:

```
void _serveTextFile(HttpRequest request) {
  String content = _getContent(request.uri.path.toString());

  request.response
    ..headers.set('Content-Type', 'text/html')
    ..statusCode = HttpStatus.OK
    ..write("""<html>
    <head><title>$BlogTitle</title></head>
    <body>
    $content
    </body>
    </html>""")
    ..close();

}
```

Once these items are set, the content for the page can be served to the requesting client, using the `response` property of the request object. Finally, the `close()` method is called, so that the client knows that the server has finished sending content.

MIME stands for **Multipurpose Internet Mail Extensions**. It is an IETF standard that is used to indicate the type of data that a file contains. This list is continually getting longer as more types of data are shared online. For more details, refer to

`http://www.iana.org/assignments/media-types/media-types.xhtml`.

Robots.txt

People with web browsers are only one type of web users. There are numerous bots and spiders out on the live Internet. To give some guidance to the nonhuman visitors, the `robots.txt` standard tells the bot whether they are welcome, and if it is a search engine, then how to index it. For the purpose of the blog server, we want to welcome search engines to index the content to bring in more readers.

The text content of the response for this will be:

```
User-agent: *
Disallow:
```

The `robots.txt` request needs to be handled and served in the same element as a regular text page:

```
void _serveRobotsFile(HttpRequest request) {
  request.response
    ..statusCode = HttpStatus.OK
    ..headers.set('Content-Type', 'text/html')
    ..write(RobotsTxt)
    ..close();
}
```

The page is served with a positive OK HTTP status.

Rendering a single blog post

The blog posts will be served on a single page for the permanent links from Uris, such as `http://127.0.0.1:8080/post6.html`, and the `_getContent` method parses the Uri path to get the ID number of the post:

```
if (path.startsWith("/post")) {
  String idfromUrl =
      path.replaceFirst("/post", "").replaceFirst(".html", "");
  int id = int.parse(idfromUrl);
  return hostedBlog.getBlogPost(id).HTML;
}
```

The output is shown in the following screenshot:

Once the ID is extracted, the blog post is retrieved and the HTML file is returned to be served as a text HTML file.

Rendering the index page

A request for the `index.html` page from this web server will show the five most recent blog posts, with the newest one at the top of the page, as shown in the following screenshot:

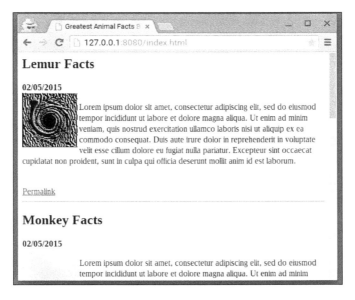

The blog posts are joined together and served as a single page:

```
String getFrontPage() {
  String frontPage = "";

  IDs.sublist(0, min(5, IDs.length)).forEach((int postID) {
    BlogPost post = getBlogPost(postID);
    frontPage += post.HTML + "<hr/>";
  });

  return frontPage;
}
```

The list of IDs processed previously is used to get the five most recent posts (or less) and the content for the posts is fetched and joined in a single HTML element.

Serving images

The HTTP header information for the PNG file type is the MIME type and the number of bytes in the image. A status code OK is also returned:

```
void _servePngFile(HttpRequest request) {
  var imgp = request.uri.path.toString();
  imgp = imgp.replaceFirst(".png", "").replaceFirst("/", "");

  image = hostedBlog.getBlogImage(int.parse(imgp));
  image.readAsBytes().then((raw) {
    request.response
      ..statusCode = HttpStatus.OK
      ..headers.set('Content-Type', 'image/png')
      ..headers.set('Content-Length', raw.length)
      ..add(raw)
      ..close();
  });
}
```

Serving an image or other binary files requires a little more information upfront, but once that is done, it is simply a matter of transferring the raw bytes and closing the connection.

Locating the file

The `getBlogImage` method of the `Blog` class returns the PNG file for display on the blog post. The `Blog` class builds up a list of image filenames when `_loadImgList` is called in the constructor. This is in the same fashion as the previously described `_loadPostList` function:

```
File getBlogImage(int index) {
   return new File(imgPaths[index]);
}
```

The ID is used as a key to get a value from a map, and the full file path is returned. The web server's Uri to a file is completely independent of the location of the filesystem, and it is the logic of the application which determines which file is to be delivered to the client.

Serving a single image file

The server is unaware of the complete structure of the web page (HTML and images) served for `index.html`. It simply returns responses to the web browser's HTTP requests in a singular manner:

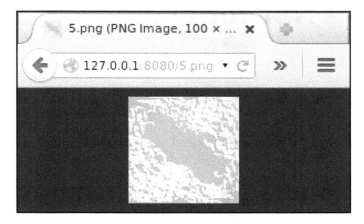

A single image can be requested directly outside the HTML page.

Serving a 404 error

Even nontechnical web users are familiar with the *404* error that indicates a page on a website cannot be found:

```
void _serve404(HttpRequest request) {
  request.response
    ..statusCode = HttpStatus.NOT_FOUND
    ..headers.set('Content-Type', 'text/html')
    ..write(page404)
    ..close();
}
```

This page is a regular text page (the constant string `page404` contains the content), and the client is further informed of the *404* status by setting the status code to `NOT_FOUND`, as shown in the following screenshot:

Let's hope that the blog server does not need to serve many of these pages!

Introducing Dart's server frameworks

The blog server in this project is written directly on top of `dart:io`, so you can see what is going on. As you might expect, there are a number of frameworks for Dart to help write server applications, so that basic tasks, such as serving text files, do not have to be implemented from scratch for every application.

These are all available at the pub package library.

Redstone

Redstone is described as "a server-side micro framework for the Dart platform". It uses simple code annotations to expose Dart functions to the Web. The Redstone `Hello World` example is very clear, and shows how annotations can hide the complexity from the developer so that they can focus on the application logic:

```
import 'package:redstone/server.dart' as app;

@app.Route("/")
helloWorld() => "Hello, World!";

main() {
  app.setupConsoleLog();
  app.start();
}
```

 You can find out more about Redstone at `http://redstonedart.org/`.

Rikulo

Rikulo modestly describes itself as a lightweight—Dart web server. It has a list of interesting features including request routing, template engine, and the **MVC (Model–view–controller)** design pattern. Rikulo Stream is the server story and its `Hello World` example to serve static content is a single line:

```
import "package:stream/stream.dart";
void main() {
  new StreamServer().start();
}
```

 You can find out more about Rikulo at `http://rikulo.org/`, where several projects are listed.

Shelf

Shelf claims that it makes it easy to create and compose web servers, and parts of web servers. Its pipeline-based model allows middleware (such as a request logger in it's `Hello World` example) to be added in:

```dart
import 'package:shelf/shelf.dart' as shelf;
import 'package:shelf/shelf_io.dart' as io;

void main() {
  var handler = const shelf.Pipeline().addMiddleware(shelf.
logRequests())
      .addHandler(_echoRequest);

  io.serve(handler, 'localhost', 8080).then((server) {
    print('Serving at http://${server.address.host}:${server.port}');
  });
}

shelf.Response _echoRequest(shelf.Request request) {
  return new shelf.Response.ok('Request for "${request.url}"');
}
```

 Find out more about Shelf at `https://github.com/dart-lang/shelf`, and as this URL suggests, this package is from the Dart team.

Deployment

After a long tough software development project, having issues to get the final product running on the live system can be extremely stressful if there is a last minute hitch. It is good to think about deployment early in the development process, so that the application is suitable for the target environment.

We will take a look at how to deploy Dart on two common environments—Windows and Unix. Of course, every individual system can vary on the details, so you may have to check for equivalent settings or programs on your system and take into account any currently running applications, such as web servers.

Dependencies

The Dart SDK itself is the key dependency for any Dart server application. The application is run via the dart command-line application, with the main.dart script passed as a parameter.

This is straightforward for an interactive session; however, for a server application, we need to run the application when there is no user logged into the machine.

 The Dart SDK is available as a separate download (not including developer tools) from
https://www.dartlang.org/downloads/.

Deploying on Unix

On a Linux or other Unix-like system, web applications can be launched within a console application called screen (lowercase s). The screen command allows the creation of other console sessions that can be left running in the background once the main session has ended.

A screen application can be created — the application is started, then the screen detached from, and the main session is ended. The web application is then left running. If a change has to be made, the detached screen can be reattached (this can be months or years later!) for any adjustments; for example, installation of a new version or configuration change.

This can be used on hosted systems where shell access (usually SSH) is allowed directly on a server.

Using the screen command

Log in to an interactive shell on your system as an appropriate user. To check whether screen is installed, run the following command to get the version and description:

```
Screen
Screen version 4.01.00devel (GNU) 2-May-06

Copyright (c) 2010 Juergen Weigert, Sadrul Habib Chowdhury
Copyright (c) 2008, 2009 Juergen Weigert, Michael Schroeder
...
```

If the program is not installed, use your package manager to install the package, simply called screen.

Launching a screen

Once `screen` application is running, press the *Enter* key and you will be at Command Prompt again. Press *Ctrl+a*, and the version screen will be displayed, showing us that we are not in a normal shell.

Use `cd` to go to the `BlogServer` folder, and start the Dart blog server:

`dart bin/main.dart`

Next, press *Ctrl+a*, *Ctrl-d* and you will see a message similar to the following one:

[detached from 398.pts-2.localhost]

You should be back in your regular terminal now. Run the command top (or any other program that lists the processes that are running on the system) to get a list of processes, and you will see Dart running in the background.

Run a web browser and navigate to the `index.html` page. The blog will be served from the editor debugging session.

To reconnect to this screen, use the command `screen -r` and you will be back in the session.

> The `screen` command is a powerful tool, but it can be a little confusing to remember which screen is in play. It is recommended that you commit keyboard shortcuts to memory for navigation.

Deploying on Windows

On Windows, server applications are usually run as Window Services, or hosted via Internet Information Services in the case of .Net applications.

It is a relatively simple operation to place the Dart `bin/main.dart` command into a batch file so that it runs with a double-click on interactive sessions. It would be best to remove this requirement for a user to be logged in if, for example, the machine is unexpectedly rebooted, or the application crashes.

Using the NSSM tool

The free tool **NSSM** (**Non-Sucking Service Manager**) (available at `http://nssm. cc/`) has a range of features to manage services. One of these is to install any application as a service, as shown in the following screenshot:

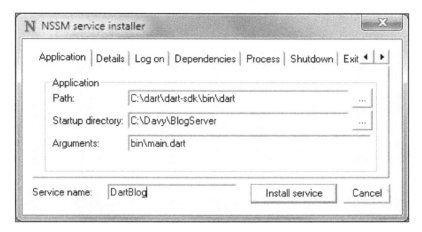

The `DartBlog` service is installed and set as automatic startup, and is run under the **Local System** account:

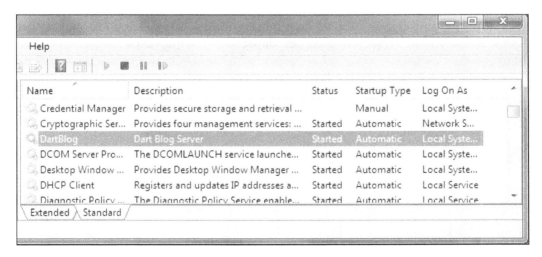

Note that the service is stopped when the first installed. Depending on what the application is does, the service will need to run under an appropriate user account, such as writing to a file, or performing other operations.

Using a Microsoft solution

Some system administrators may be happier if they use a more official Microsoft-based solution.

As an alternative, Microsoft provides a tool called **srvany**, which is service that is used to launch other applications. It is an older tool (dating back to NT4 Resource Kit), but is commonly used for this purpose. For more information, refer to `https://support.microsoft.com/en-us/kb/137890`.

Load testing

It is good to know the limits of an application long before you ever reach them. The `HttpClientRequest` function can be used to create requests to the blog server, and the `HttpClientResponse` function can be used to receive incoming data from the blog server.

The `statusCode` property will be checked to ensure that the page request was successfully handled by the server.

Building a simple load tool

A simple benchmark for the blog server would be the time taken to serve 1000 files. The `getUrl` method triggers the actual request with the first `then` clause, closing the request to the server. The following `then` clause handles the actual response from the server.

This method can be used to monitor a live website and perhaps trigger a notification if a status other than `HttpStatus.OK` is received:

```
import 'dart:io';

main() {
  print("Starting...");

  var url = "http://127.0.0.1:8080/index.html";
  var hc = new HttpClient();
  var watch = new Stopwatch();
  int attemptedRequests = 1000;

  print("Starting testing...");
  watch.start();
```

```
for (int i=0;i<attemptedRequests;i++)
{
  hc.getUrl(Uri.parse(url))
    .then((HttpClientRequest request) => request.close())
    .then((HttpClientResponse response) {
      if (response.statusCode==HttpStatus.OK)
        print("$i, ${response.statusCode}, ${watch.elapsed.
inMilliseconds}");
    });
}
}
```

The `Stopwatch` class can be used to measure the time taken and reported to standard output via a print statement. As the responses arrive asynchronously, the status is printed after each response. The request number, status code, and elapsed time are printed with a comma between each value, so that the data can easily be manipulated in a spreadsheet application.

Try putting a `print` statement directly after the loop has finished and you will see the print run before the first response is received from the server (or soon after).

On my modest Linux laptop, the server was able to serve `index.html` 2000 times in 3.8 seconds—not too bad! Try experimenting with the request number; however, you are likely to hit a limit on open files, as this simple benchmark fires many simultaneous requests.

Summary

We saw how the `dart:io` package can help build an HTTP server very quickly, and how frameworks can make this even easier. Using some simple processing of the request string, we can do more than serve the files flatly from the filesystem, such as serving the most recent entries on the front page.

The freedom of being out of the browser allows the manipulation of the filesystem. Despite not being on the Web, there is still good support for HTTP operations, which we used to test the performance of the server. Dart server applications can easily be installed on industry-standard host operating systems in a standard manner.

Our blog server is off to a good start. To progress, it needs to do more for the author, the reader, and the growing number of intelligent web crawlers and bots out on the Internet. We will provide an editor to create posts, cache requests to serve pages faster, and expose the posts in other data formats.

6

Blog Server Advanced

One reason I encourage people to blog is that the act of doing it stretches your
available vocabulary and hones a new voice.

– Seth Godin

Blogs (a shortened form of the term "web logs") grew from simple homepages and made it faster to get content online for casual users. They also took care of some of the metainformation and publishing that allows content to spread around the Internet and can be found by machines and human consumers.

On the server-side, Dart has greater access to the filesystem and is not limited by the capabilities of a browser. This chapter explores these features more as we add more features to the blog server.

Logging

Web servers such as **Apache** and **IIS** track a visitor's web browser usage, which helps webmasters understand how visitors use their site and how many people view the pages. This good practice also helps web developers find problems in their site and helps the developers of a web server software diagnose issues.

 For general-purpose logging in your Dart applications, take a look at the logging package, which is authored by the Dart team and is available at

https://pub.dartlang.org/packages/logging.

Writing text files

With `dart:io`, we already read files from the file system, and writing operates in a similar manner, as follows:

```
import 'dart:io';

void main() {
  File myfile = new File("example.txt");
  myfile.writeAsStringSync("Hello Word!");
}
```

This demonstrates the synchronous version of the function, with `writeAsString` being the asynchronous version.

Open the `log.dart` file in this chapter's project. For this, take a look at the following code snippet:

```
void log(HttpRequest request) {
  String entry = getLogEntry(request);
  File logstore = new File("accesslog.txt");
  logstore.writeAsStringSync(entry, mode: FileMode.APPEND);
}
```

To record the web access request to the disk, the log entries will have to be accumulative so that the entries are written with the APPEND mode passed as a named parameter.

Extracting request information

The `HttpRequest` object and `headers` property expose metadata from the request to the client. For example, the `headers` property can give the host and port number. The user-agent identifies which program or web browser was used when making the request, as shown in the following code snippet:

```
String getLogEntry(HttpRequest request) {

  //USER_AGENT
  HttpHeaders headers = request.headers;
  String reqUri = "${headers.host},${headers.port}${request.uri.
toString()}";
  String entry =
      " ${request.connectionInfo.remoteAddress.address}, $reqUri,
${headers[HttpHeaders.USER_AGENT]}\r\n";

  return (new DateTime.now()).toString() + entry;
}
```

The `remoteAddress` getter (IP address) can be used to track who was browsing and from which part of the world. Log entries to request the `index.html` blog would look as follows:

```
2015-05-17 17:03:48.496 127.0.0.1, 127.0.0.1,8080/index.html,
[Mozilla/5.0 (X11; CrOS x86_64 6812.88.0) AppleWebKit/537.36 (KHTML,
like Gecko) Chrome/42.0.2311.153 Safari/537.36]
2015-05-17 17:03:49.177 127.0.0.1, 127.0.0.1,8080/6.png, [Mozilla/5.0
(X11; CrOS x86_64 6812.88.0) AppleWebKit/537.36 (KHTML, like Gecko)
Chrome/42.0.2311.153 Safari/537.36]
2015-05-14 18:52:45.690 127.0.0.1, 127.0.0.1,8080/favicon.ico,
[NetSurf/2.9 (Linux; x86_64)]
```

Browsers will request the page that is browsed to by the user and also other assets such as `favicon.ico` (the small square graphic that is often shown in the URL bar of a web browser or on a bookmark).

A blog editor

A blog will have an administration section that will allow us to update the blog using the Web. This will be accessible through the address `http://localhost:8080/admin`, using the `admin` login as the username and `Password1` as the password (both case sensitive).

 Never ever ever use such a simple login in a real application!

The admin section of the blog's website will consist of web forms. The forms will use the `post` method so that the blog server will have to detect this correctly in the `_handleRequest` method of the `BlogServerApp` class to handle the request. This is exposed by the `method` property of the `request` object, as shown in the following code snippet:

```
if (request.method == 'POST') {
  _handleFormPost(request);
}
```

`POST` requests still have a URI associated with them, allowing a decision over how to handle the input. For detailed information, let's take a look at the following code snippet:

```
void _handleFormPost(HttpRequest request) {
  if (request.uri.path == "/login") _performLogin(request);
  if (request.uri.path == "/add") _performNewPost(request);
}
```

The handling of the login process and the new blog post are rather different.

Password protection

The /admin path serves the web form that allows the entry of the username and password required to access the admin features, as shown in the following screenshot:

The username and password will be verified, and if they are correct, the form to add a blog post will be shown to you. Let's take a look at the following code snippet:

```
void _performLogin(HttpRequest request) {
  request.listen((List<int> buffer) {
    String page = _checkAdminLogin(buffer);

    request.response
      ..statusCode = HttpStatus.OK
      ..headers.set('Content-Type', 'text/html')
      ..write(page)
      ..close();
  }, onDone: () => request.response.close());
}
```

The checkAdminLogin method performs the checking of the login details and returns either the web form or a message stating that the login attempt has failed.

Encryption

Security is an important feature of any administration feature of a web application. We will not want to store the password on the site in plain text! A typical way to store the password is a one-way hash, which makes the password hard to crack even if the attacker has the hash value.

The `crypto` package provides a range of encryption options. The `SHA` algorithm will be used for this purpose for the blog, as follows:

```
String _checkAdminLogin(List<int> buffer) {
  var sha = new SHA256();
  sha.add(buffer);
  var digest = sha.close();
  String hex = CryptoUtils.bytesToHex(digest);
  String page = "";

  if (hex != expectedHash) {
    page = wrongPassword;
  } else {
    page = addForm;
  }

  return page;
}
```

Conveniently, the input for the hash is a `List<int>` list, and this is exactly what is received from the web form input into the request's `listen` handler. The `SHA256` algorithm simply takes a body of data and then has the `close` method called to return the calculated hash.

 SHA stands for Secure Hash Algorithm. The 256 refers to the word size. If you have ever installed a package on a Linux system, then you have used **SHA-256**. The crypto-currency Bitcoin also uses SHA for some of its operations.

As both the username and password have to be correct, the entire input from the form can simply be hashed and compared against a previously calculated value. For easy storage, the hash is converted to a hexadecimal string, as follows:

```
const String expectedHash = "bdf252c8385e7c4ae76bca280acd8d44
f85d7fdb56f1bfb44f5749ff549ba2f6";
```

This is stored as a constant in `content.dart`.

Handling more complex forms

Of course, form handling is not always as straightforward as the login page. Typically, form elements need to be split apart and handled separately. The served page after logging into the administration page will allow the user to add a new post to the blog. The user will supply the post title and body text and the post ID number and date will be generated by the application, as shown in the next screenshot:

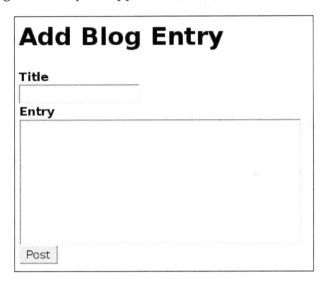

Processing the form

The _performNewPost method calls the getFormData utility function to split the data into a more manageable list. This rather low-level web programming is typically wrapped up by most Dart web frameworks, as shown in the following code snippet:

```
List _getFormData(List<int> buffer) {
    var encodedData = new String.fromCharCodes(buffer);
    List pieces = encodedData.split("&");
    List data = [];
    List finalData = [];
```

```
pieces
    .forEach((dateItem) =>
        data.add(dateItem.substring(dateItem.indexOf("=") + 1)));

data.forEach(
    (encodedItem) => finalData.add(Uri.decodeQueryComponent(encod
edItem)));

return finalData;
}
```

The data is first split into data from each control, and then the data is decoded using the Uri.decodeQueryComponent component to the raw data before it is returned to the caller.

Saving data to a disk

The data has been processed to a manageable list, so now we only need to construct a blog post and save it to the filesystem. This is carried out by the _performNewPost method of the BlogServerApp method. Let's take a look at the following code snippet:

```
List formData = _getFormData(buffer);
String newID = hostedBlog.getNextPostID();
String filename = "$newID.txt";
var p = path.join("content", "posts");
p = path.join(p, filename);

File postFile = new File(p);
String post = BlogPost.createBlogPost(formData[0], formData[1]);
postFile.writeAsStringSync(post);
```

The blog object returns the next free PostId, which is used in the file name, and the full path is constructed using path.join from the path package. The createBlogPost static method on the BlogPost class is used to add extra data in the defined format. This is written to the constructed path using the synchronous write function.

Serving a default graphic

This version of the add form does not allow a user to set a graphic file, which each post requires. If the blog post ID is 8, then 8.png will be requested. Rather than not loading any file, a default image (default.png) will be loaded up. Let's take a look at the following screenshot:

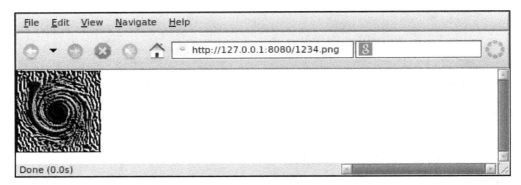

If the file is not found on the filesystem (such as the fictitious 1234.png image!), then 6.png is loaded and served instead, as shown in the following code snippet:

```
File getBlogImage(int index) {
  String path;
  if (imgPaths.containsKey(index)) {
    path = imgPaths[index];
  } else {
    path = _pathDefaultImg;
  }

  return new File(path);
}
```

This is implemented by simply testing the imgPaths map for the requested index variable. If the key is not present in the imgPaths map, the default image path is used.

Refreshing the blog

The content of the blog is read when the blog server is started. As this content has now changed with the new blog post, this list must be refreshed using the BlogServerApp method called initBlog, as follows:

```
initBlog() async {
  _cache = {};
  IDs = new List<int>();
  postPaths = new Map<int, String>();
  imgPaths = new Map<int, String>();
  await _loadPostList();
  _loadImgList();
}
```

The `BlogServerApp` and `_performNewPost` methods perform the task of calling `initBlog` before serving the new post, as follows:

```
hostedBlog.initBlog();

req.response
  ..statusCode = HttpStatus.OK
  ..headers.set('Content-Type', 'text/html')
  ..redirect(new Uri(path: "post$newID.html"))
  ..close();
```

Once the blog is reinitialized, the application serves the new blog post to the user as a single page.

Caching

The serving of content in the first iteration of the web server was rather inefficient—I hope you noticed! On every GET request, the blog source file is read from the disk and is processed. To gain some efficiency, we can use a map added to the `Blog` class as a field. Let's take a look at the following code snippet for more information:

```
BlogPost getBlogPost(int index) {
if (!_cache.containsKey(index)) {
  _cache[index] = new BlogPost(postPaths[index], index);
}
return _cache[index];
}
```

The map object uses the blog `index` as a key and the resultant blog post as the value. This cache is kept in the memory so that if the blog server application is stopped and restarted, new requests will not initially come from the cache.

Caching of content in web applications is quite an art. For example, a cache could be put in place at the request level for both entire pages and images. The underlying operating system will also cache files in memory, making operations much faster on subsequent requests.

As ever, a memory cache is just one tool that may or may not improve a particular application. Benchmarking a performance and finding the bottleneck that needs caching is critical for a high-performance application.

The cache is something that must be remembered when the content is refreshed and when a new blog post is added. A simple strategy is to set the _cache object to { } (an empty map), relying on the first display of the post to fill the cache.

Watching the filesystem

It is very convenient to update a web form from any computer. It may also be useful to update it purely from the filesystem so that a standard text editor can be used or we can have the blog post content entirely automated.

The watcher package provides the functionality needed for this feature. This package is authored by the Dart team and is typically of the Dart philosophy of being a small focused library. The DirectoryWatcher class takes a path and notifies via events if any files have added, removed, or modified.

The Blog class constructor configures the path that is going to be watched by the DirectoryWatcher. Let's take a look at the following screenshot:

```
DirectoryWatcher _changeMonitor;

Blog(this._pathPosts, this._pathImgs) {
  initBlog();
  _changeMonitor = new DirectoryWatcher(this._pathPosts);
  _changeMonitor.events.listen((watchEvent) => initBlog());
}
```

The actual details of the change are not important for the blog, so the initBlog method will be called to reset the entire site.

In the content folder of this chapter's sample code, there is an unpublished blog post with the 7.txt filename. Start the main.dart blog server located in the bin folder and go to the index.html page. Open the file manager on your system and locate the 7.txt file. Move this file into the posts folder and refresh the web page. A new blog post should appear at the top of the page, as shown in the following screenshot:

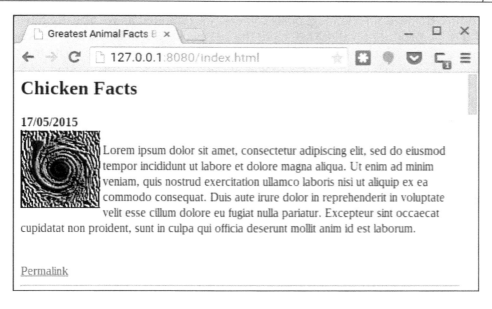

Return to the folder and move the `7.txt` file out of the posts folder. Refresh the web browser again and the most recent post on **Chicken Facts** will have gone.

XML feed generation

For blog reader's search and syndication, a blog needs to produce an RSS feed. RSS is an XML specification that lists blog posts in a specified format as separate items that are simple to process.

In late 1990s, there were many attempts to create a syndication format for the Web. Dan Libby and Ramanathan V. Guha from Netscape created the RDF site summary format in 1999 for use in the My.Netscape.Com portal. The RDF specification was refined and eventually became RSS.

The competing (and in my opinion, much superior!) feed format is Atom. Atom was developed to fix the shortcomings of RSS has not gained much traction with simple RSS and web services used for more advanced applications.

As well as blog and news publications, RSS is also established as the standard format for podcasting and its supporting clients and tools.

The full specification is available at `https://validator.w3.org/feed/docs/rss2.html`.

To produce the feed for the blog, posts can easily be iterated as we already have a list of IDs. To produce a valid XML feed, the xml package will be used. This is not part of the SDK and is an open source library, which has become a favorite for XML creation and processing in Dart. There was at one time an XML processing package in the SDK, but the xml package was improved so quickly that it made more sense to make it the standard package. Let's have a look at the following code snippet for more information:

```dart
String getRSSFeed() {
  var RssXb = new XmlBuilder();
  RssXb.processing('xml', 'version="1.0"');

  RssXb.element('rss', attributes: {'version': '1.0'}, nest: () {
    RssXb.element('channel', nest: () {
      IDs.forEach((int postID) {
        BlogPost post = getBlogPost(postID);
        RssXb.element('item', nest: () {
          RssXb.element('pubDate', nest: () {
            RssXb.text(post._date);
          });
          RssXb.element('title', nest: () {
            RssXb.text(post._title);
          });
          RssXb.element('link', nest: () {
            RssXb.text("http://127.0.0.1:8080/post${post._id}.
html");
          });
        }); //item
      });
    }); //channel
  }); //rss

  var xml = RssXb.build();
  return xml.toXmlString(pretty: true);
}
```

Elements are added in a nested fashion here, which reflects the RSS structure. Once the data structure is put together, the build method constructs the XML structure, and finally, it is converted into a string.

For simple XML, it is tempting just to concatenate strings. However, an XML library can provide facilities such as character encoding, validation, and formatting ,which are well worth the slightly more verbose code on the smaller use cases.

As it will be viewed by human beings as well as computers, the optional name parameter option `pretty` is set to true for a neatly formatted output, as shown in the following example:

```
<?xml version="1.0"?>
<rss version="1.0">
  <channel>
    <item>
      <pubDate>02/05/2015</pubDate>
      <title>Lemur Facts</title>
      <link>http://127.0.0.1:8080/post6.html</link>
    </item>
  ...
```

The RSS feed is served to `http://127.0.0.1:8080/feed.xml` and can be viewed directly in most web browsers.

Serving the RSS

The RSS feed can be served as any other text file, though the headers will need to be set to assist the client application. Let's take a look at the following code snippet for more information:

```
void _serveRSSFeed(HttpRequest request) {
  request.response
    ..statusCode = HttpStatus.OK
    ..headers.set('Content-Type', 'application/rss+xml')
    ..write(hostedBlog.getRSSfeed())
    ..close();
}
```

The content type is set to `application/rss+xml`, which triggers the XML display in the browser. Otherwise, it may attempt to display the content as HTML.

The JSON feed generation

Serving a **JSON (JavaScript Object Notation)** feed is a useful alternative to XML, as it requires the transfer of less data and is often easier and faster to deal with rather than dealing with XPath. The `getJSONfeed` method is part of the `Blog` class, shown as follows:

```
String getJSONFeed() {
  List posts = new List();
  IDs.forEach((int postID) {
    BlogPost post = getBlogPost(postID);
    Map jsonPost = {};
    jsonPost["id"] = post._id;
    jsonPost["date"] = post._date;
    jsonPost["title"] = post._title;
    jsonPost["url"] = "http://127.0.0.1:8080/post${post._id}.html";
    posts.add(jsonPost);
  });
  return JSON.encode(posts);
}
```

This method follows the same approach as RSS, with the main data structure being a list this time and the items being entries in that list. The list can be converted to JSON using the `JSON.encode` method from `dart:convert`:

```
[
...
{"id" : 6,
  "date" : "02/05/2015",
  "title" : "Lemur Facts",
  "url" : "http://127.0.0.1:8080/post6.html"},
...
]
```

 The JSON feed is served to `http://127.0.0.1:8080/feed.json` and can be viewed directly in most web browsers.

Serving the JSON

The serving of JSON requires not only the correct type to be specified, but also the security needs to be dealt with for the consumption of this data feed from another web domain:

```
    void _serveJsonFile(HttpRequest request) {
    request.response
      ..statusCode = HttpStatus.OK
      ..headers.set('Content-Type', 'application/json')
      ..headers.add("Access-Control-Allow-Origin", "*")
      ..headers.add(
          "Access-Control-Allow-Methods",
  "POST,GET,DELETE,PUT,OPTIONS")
      ..write(hostedBlog.getJSONFeed())
      ..close();
  }
```

The content type is set to `application/json`, which triggers the XML display in the browser. The access control (CORS) is set to allow any origin and a set of HTTP verbs.

> **Cross-origin resource sharing** (**CORS**) is a technology that permits restricted resources, such as scripts to be requested from other web domains. For example, a news site wants to request the headlines in the JSON format from a blog to display them.
>
> By default, resources can only be loaded from the same domain. CORS allows specific resources, and actions (HTTP verbs) on those resources such as GET, POST, and so on to be shared. So, we may be happy to share our headlines, but not our login validation scripts.

Consuming the JSON feed

JSON has certainly established itself as the modern web data format, being lightweight to both produce and consume. To explore the JSON feature from end to end, we will detour briefly from the server-side and return to the client-side Dart in order to exercise the blog's JSON data feed. For this, take a look at the following code snippet:

Open the example project `BlogJsonClient` of this chapter. This a simple web project which acts as a client to the Blog server JSON feed. For this client to operate, the blog server must also be running.

```
void main() {
var jsonSrc = "http://127.0.0.1:8080/feed.json";
 HttpRequest.getString(jsonSrc).then((String data) {
    List decoded = JSON.decode(data);
    decoded.forEach((post) {
      querySelector('#output').children.add(new LIElement()
        ..append(new AnchorElement()
          ..href = post['url']
          ..text = "${post['date']} ${post['title']}"));
    }); //for
  }); //then
}
```

The consumer of the JSON feed does not need to be aware of the CORS settings in any way. It simply makes an HTTP request to the appropriate URL to receive the JSON data or other resource. The request must meet the CORS requirements, such as the origin or HTTP verb to receive the desired response. Let's take a look at the following screenshot:

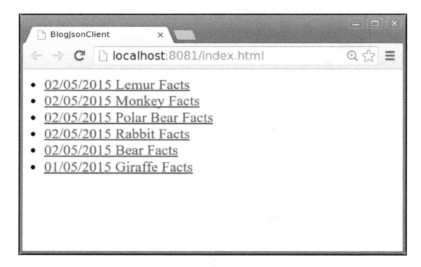

Here, the HttpRequest class has a static method to return a remote resource as Future<String>, which is handled asynchronously in the then clause.

JSON is then iterated and the **LI** elements (**List Items**) are added to the DOM structure of the web page.

Static generation

Web hosting facilities vary greatly from provider to provider. The ability to run programs and install software is not universally available. Static generation of websites has become more popular with the ability to run small simple virtual machines on the cloud.

The advantages are very clear, there is not maintenance on software or a database to maintain, making the system very secure and also very fast to serve. It is not suitable for all applications, though. Blogging is one where static generation may make sense.

Freezing the website

In this chapter's project, there is a `staticgen.dart` file in the `bin` folder. This is a standalone program that generates a static HTML file of the front page of the blog. Note that the `main` function is marked with the `async` keyword and is missing the `void` keyword.

Introducing the await and async keywords

The `await` and `async` keywords were introduced in Dart 1.9.4 in order to simplify asynchronous operations. Consider the following call to a method that returns `Future`:

```
obj.method().then(handlerFunction)
```

This is fine for the post part, but what if things get more complicated and `handlerFunction` returns a future too?

```
obj.method().then(handlerFunction).then(handlerFunction2);
```

Things are starting to get complicated already—debugging is not straightforward. Ideally, we would want to deal with one part of the chain at a time and hold up the execution of statements until a desired operation is complete. This is what `await` allows:

```
var f1 = await obj.aMethod();
var result = await f1.aMethod();
```

Functions and methods to be called with `await` return `Future`. They must also be declared as `async` in the method's header, as does the function using the `await` call:

```
class Foo{
    Future<int> aMethod() async {
    return await aFunction();
    }
}
```

The `async` and `await` keywords simplify the code, particularly if in-line functions are being used, and they also make the asynchronous code much more readable.

Joining file paths

Most computer users have hit the issue with forward and backward slashes being used on paths in Unix-style (`/home/davymitchell/`) and Windows operating systems (`c:\users\davymitchell\`):

```
var contPath = path.join(Directory.current.path, "content");
var srcPath = path.join(contPath, "posts");
var imgPath = path.join(contPath, "img");
```

The `path` package provides a cross-platform method `join` to join folder and file names.

Creating an output folder

The output files will be placed in a folder named `staticoutput` on the current path. The existence of this folder will be tested, and if it is not present, the folder will be created. Let's take a look at the following code snippet:

```
main() async {
  var contPath = path.join(Directory.current.path, "content");
  var srcPath = path.join(contPath, "posts");
  var imgPath = path.join(contPath, "img");

  Blog staticBlog = new Blog(srcPath, imgPath);
  await staticBlog.initBlog();
  print(Directory.current);

  // Create output directory if it does not exist.
  var outDir = new Directory('staticoutput');
  var staticPath = path.join(Directory.current.path, 'staticoutput');
  if (!await outDir.exists()) {
    outDir.create();
  }
```

```
    // Write out main page.
    var outPath = path.join(staticPath, "index.html");
    var pageContent = staticBlog.getFrontPage();
    File indexPage = new File(outPath);
    await indexPage.writeAsString(pageContent, mode: FileMode.WRITE);

    // Return success exit code.
    exit(0);
}
```

The outcome of the asynchronous method exists and is waited upon before the program continues.

Generating the front page

In *Chapter 5, A Blog Server*, there is a version of Blog Server called initBlog from the constructor. It has been moved to a post object creation initialization call so that await can be used. Methods and functions marked as async cannot be called from constructors. The use of async simplifies the _loadPostList method, as there is much less nesting, as shown in the following code snippet:

```
_loadPostList() async {
  print("Loading from $_pathPosts");
  Directory blogContent = new Directory(_pathPosts);

  var postsSrc = await blogContent.list();

  await postsSrc.forEach((File f) {
    String postFilename = path.basenameWithoutExtension(f.path);
    int id = int.parse(postFilename);
    IDs.add(id);
    postPaths[id] = f.path;
  });

  IDs.sort();
  IDs = IDs.reversed.toList();
}
```

Previously, the posts were loaded and the blog was set up asynchronously.

If you are looking for some good blogs on Dart programming, a good place to start is http://www.dartosphere.org/, which is a blog aggregator or planet-style website with news and resources from various sources.

Writing the static version

Now that the page content is available at a determinable time, it can be written out on a disk using the writeAsString method. The FileMode.WRITE permission will overwrite any existing file, hence is suitable for updates. Let's take a look at the following code snippet:

```
var outPath = path.join(staticPath, "index.html");
var pageContent = staticBlog.getFrontPage();
File indexPage = new File(outPath);
indexPage.writeAsStringSync(pageContent, mode:FileMode.WRITE);

exit(0);
```

The last line returns an exit code to the OS when the program completes, with 0 being the convention for success. This function does not wait for any pending operations, closing the program immediately.

Load testing revisited

The initial load testing application was rather limited, and though of use, it did not give a realistic picture with so many requests thrown at once at the server application without waiting for a response.

Updating the load tester

The new version of the load testing application will make a single HTTP call and await the result before calling the next. This takes place in the main.dart source file. Note that the main function itself in now marked as async. The await command is used in the calling loop of the main function, as follows:

```
main() async {
  print("Starting...");

  var url = "http://127.0.0.1:8080/index.html";
  var hc = new HttpClient();
  var watch = new Stopwatch();
  int attemptedRequests = 200;
```

```
print("Starting testing...");
watch.start();

for (int i = 0; i < attemptedRequests; i++) {
    await callWebPage(hc, url, i, watch);
}

watch.stop();
print("${watch.elapsed.inMilliseconds}");
}
```

The `callWebPage` method needs to be marked as `async` too, as `await` will be used twice:

```
callWebPage(HttpClient webClient, String targetURL, int requestNumber,
    Stopwatch watch) async {
  HttpClientRequest request;
  HttpClientResponse response;
  request = await webClient.getUrl(Uri.parse(targetURL));
  response = await request.close();
  print("$requestNumber, ${response.statusCode}, ${watch.elapsed.
inMilliseconds}");
}
```

The two operations of unknown duration, the URL fetch and closing of the response, are waited upon before the output to the screen is processed.

Summary

The server side opens up many facilities of the filesystem to save the content directly from the application, supplying content for web servers and metadata, such as log files.

Dart has the facilities to create, serve, and consume the modern web formats in the web client and on the server. We saw how quickly a specialized web server can be put together. You are now very familiar with using Dart packages outside the core SDK to implement vital application features.

The asynchronous facilities allow responsive applications to be written, and `await`/`async` helps us write clear code and bring asynchronous tasks together so that we operate them in a synchronous manner.

Our next, and largest, project will be end-to-end Dart. In this chapter, we explored how to build on the server aspects. Instead of the local filesystem, we will reach out to databases and web services to build a real-time display.

7
Live Data Collection

"It is a capital mistake to theorize before one has data."

- Sherlock Holmes

Most people in the IT world are familiar with the phrase **Garbage In, Garbage Out** (**GIGO**). If bad data goes into a system, the output will be wrong too. A source of good data should always be used, and systems need to be robust enough to handle users or other systems' 'garbage'. Specifications and standards can help, but there will always be exceptions and gray areas.

One of the most baffling statements I have heard in my career was from a customer with a software data input issue: 'we have our own ISO standard'!

Kicking off the earthquake monitoring system

The next series of chapters in the book will be built around a single project from several different perspectives. A real-world data source with earthquake information about the planet we live on will be tracked, recorded and displayed.

It is quite ambitious and there will be a lot of Dart along the way. It is surprising how much activity there is in the Earth's crust—perhaps you could blog or write a presentation on seismology using the output of our projects so far!

The project for this section is called `QuakeMonitorFS`—make sure that you select the project with the name ending FS and not DB. The FS version saves to the filesystem while the DB version saves to the database. We will first look at the filesystem storage version, and then move on to the database version.

Introducing the data source

The data source for the application is a web service provided by the **United States Geological Survey (USGS)** Earthquake Hazards Program. There is a wealth of information on their website http://earthquake.usgs.gov/ including some continually updated data feeds from all around the world.

The data feeds that are of most interest for Dart programmers are in a particular JSON format.

Exploring the GeoJSON format

GeoJSON is a format for recording geographic data structures, which includes support of geometric definitions, such as points and polygons. For example, the location of an earthquake's epicenter (point) and the area affected (polygon). Part of the GeoJSON can look as follows:

```
{
 "type":"Point",
 "coordinates":[122.3818333,45.0686667,12.9]
}
,
"id":"uw61022191"
```

 The previous example is a small excerpt from the feed that reports all earthquakes in the past hour (http://earthquake.usgs.gov/earthquakes/feed/v1.0/summary/all_hour.geojson). Take a moment to look at this feed and get a feel for the type of data this format contains.

To kick off this project, we will create a data-monitoring application that will record information from this feed. As this program will be running over a long period, we will want to add a logging feature to ensure it is running smoothly.

Fetching and recording the data

The main function in bin/main.dart will prompt the data to be downloaded each minute using an instance of the DataMonitor class. There are *1440* minutes in a day and the data files average at around *2k,* so 3 megabytes of disk space a day is practical:

```
main() async {
  setupLogging();

  DataMonitor quakeMon = new DataMonitor();
```

```
    Duration updateInterval = new Duration(seconds: 60);

    new Timer.periodic(updateInterval, quakeMon.fetchData);
  }
```

The main function is marked async, which gives you a clue that the implementation will make use of the await feature. The call to setupLogging will be covered in the next section of this chapter.

The implementation of DataMonitor is in lib/quakemonitorfs.dart, which contains the key method fetchData:

```
    fetchData(Timer timerFetch) async {
      try {
        var outDir = new Directory('data');
        if (!await outDir.exists()) {
          outDir.create();
        }

        log.info("Calling web service...");
        HttpClientRequest req = await geoClient.getUrl(Uri.
parse(dataUrl));
        HttpClientResponse resp = await req.close();
        String latestFilePath = path.join('data', latestFilename);
        await resp.pipe(new File(latestFilePath).openWrite());
        String fileContents = await new File(latestFilePath).
readAsString();

        var dataset = await JSON.decode(fileContents);

        int newId = int.parse(dataset['metadata']['generated'].
toString());

        if (idPreviousFetch != newId) {
          idPreviousFetch = newId;
          var f = new File(path.join('data', '${newId}.txt'));
          await f.writeAsString(dataset.toString());
          log.fine("Saved $newId - ${dataset.toString()}");
        }
      } catch (exception, stacktrace) {
        log.severe("Exception fetching JSON.", exception, stacktrace);
      }
    }
```

Nearly every other line has an `await`! The program only has to process information every minute or so, therefore it does not require a responsive structure and a more linear approach is sufficient, though the code is still `asynchronous`.

The remote resource is processed first and the response closed off. The JSON string returned can be put straight into a file. Once this is completed, the `fileContents` variable is populated with the data from the file, which is then parsed by the JSON to return an object into the dataset.

The `Id` of the response is checked so that the same response is not saved twice. Note that the generated `Id` may be different, while the content is the same. The feed is more of a snapshot than a steady stream.

The data is saved off to the data folder using the id of the fetch as a text (`.txt`) file. To give some feedback, the id and JSON are written to the log file via the call to `qlog.fine`.

Logging

I reached many points of difficulty in my early software projects where the only thing left to do was to resort to logging, to figure out what was going on. Soon I grew to enjoy logging and made it a key point when starting a new project. It is an extra pair of eyes to help you test—especially when you are not looking, such as when running a data collector continuously.

The Dart package `logging` provides facilities for logging, however it does not do anything useful with the output, or to put it another way, the handling of the storage of the logging is entirely in the hands of the application.

A simple example of logging

Open up this chapter's `Logging` folder, which is a standalone example containing a range of logging:

```
Logger log = new Logger('DataMonitor');

Logger.root.level = Level.ALL;
Logger.root.onRecord.listen((LogRecord rec) {
  String logMessage = '${rec.level.name}\t${rec.time}\t\t${rec.
message}';
  String exceptionMessage = '';
  if (rec.error != null) {
    print("$logMessage \t${rec.error.message}");
    print(exceptionMessage);
```

```
      print(rec.stackTrace);
    } else {
      print("$logMessage");
    }
  });
```

The `Logger` object is initialized and the `level` property set to `Level.ALL`. Setting this property gives control over the detail of logging occurring. The custom handler for an incoming log message simply prints it to standard output. Other possibilities are writing to disk, database, or a network socket:

```
log.info("This is my first logging program in Dart");
log.fine("Level 1 detail.");
log.finer("Level 2 detail.");
log.finest("Level 3 detail.");
log.shout("Something bad.");
```

The `Logger` class has numerous methods for logging out at different levels, and this also helps produce readable code. By having levels of logging, this can assist with analysis of the logs file. For example, if an application's logs are being looked at to get a general overview of what is going on, the `info` level of logging would be examined. If a low-level bug is occurring, the approach would be to check the logging down to the `finest` level. Each method also allows the passing of an `Exception` and a stack trace:

```
try {
  throw new Exception("We have a problem!");
} catch (exception, stackTrace) {
  log.severe("Something really bad.", exception, stackTrace);
}
```

The name passed to the `Logger` constructor, in this case `DataMonitor`, identifies a unique object. Any other scope can declare a `Logger` object with the same name, and the same instance will be returned.

Data monitor logging

For the `QuakeMonitorFS`, the application launch and the calls to the web service will be recorded. Network connections are not perfect, so we will want to know if the program has not been able to access the web service. Lets have a look at the following code snippet:

```
Logger log;

setupLogging() {
```

```
log = new Logger('DataMonitor');
Logger.root.level = Level.ALL;
Logger.root.onRecord.listen((LogRecord rec) {
  var entry = '${rec.level.name}\t${rec.time}\t\t${rec.message}\n';
  File logStore = new File("datamonlog.txt");
  logStore.writeAsStringSync(entry, mode: FileMode.APPEND);
});
  log.info('Earthquake Monitor - Data fetcher. Starting...');
}
```

The logging is set up in `bin/main.dart` and the output appended to a text file. Note that this is not saved to the data sub-folder, as it may get lost with all the data files.

In the `fetchData` method of the `DataMonitor` class, the `Logger` object is set up in the constructor, and key events will be noted. The different levels of logging are used (info, fine, severe, and so on), which would allow an operator of the program to adjust the level of logging to the desired level.

Saving to the database

The data collector application currently writes to the filesystem. While this is useful for archiving, it makes it difficult and slow to access and query any sort of analysis or display.

If you are not experienced with databases, here is a very rapid introduction! Databases are collections of data in a structured form. These are accessed and managed via a database management system. You may have heard of **SQL Server**, **MySQL**, **Hadoop** or **Oracle**.

Databases are typically accessed using a language called SQL to read and write records from the database. Data is usually organized into tables, and each table is made up of records. Each table has a set columns defined as data types — it is similar to variables in a programming language. SQL is strong on sorting, grouping, and working with sets of data.

SQL can be stored in the database in a number of forms, with the most common being a stored procedure that can add/ remove and update data, and perform some processing.

Connecting to a database almost always requires a login and may be on a remote computer. This is sometimes referred to as a connection string. It behaves much like a network connection.

Installing a database system

There are numerous database systems available and you probably already have your favorite one! For the purposes of this book, the database used will be **PostgreSQL** as it is free, open source, and available for all the major operating systems. Also it is one of the easiest databases to install, so we can spend more time writing Dart.

PostgreSQL is a powerful, open-source, object-relational database system with a 15-year heritage behind it.

It is a first-class product and is used by big names in industry and government, such as Yahoo and the United Nations. It complies strongly with SQL language standards and can cope with database tables up to a maximum size of *32* terabytes.

PostgreSQL can be downloaded from `http://www.postgresql.org/` for Mac, Linux, and Windows, and is available via most Linux distribution package managers. Also on the PostgreSQL download page, there are numerous virtual machine images available that just need to be downloaded and turned on.

The examples for this book assume that the database installation is the same machine that the software is run from. Adjusting the connection string will allow connection to remote machines.

Using PostgreSQL from Dart

The package `postgresql` provides a very capable PostgreSQL database driver to use from the Dart program. It is a third-party package that is well regarded, and has had contributions from the Dart team.

The project for this section is called `QuakeMonitorDB` and the fetching is identical to the filesystem version.

Introducing the pgAdmin GUI

For a graphical tool to access the database, use pgAdmin (also available for Mac, Windows and Linux) `http://www.pgadmin.org/download/`

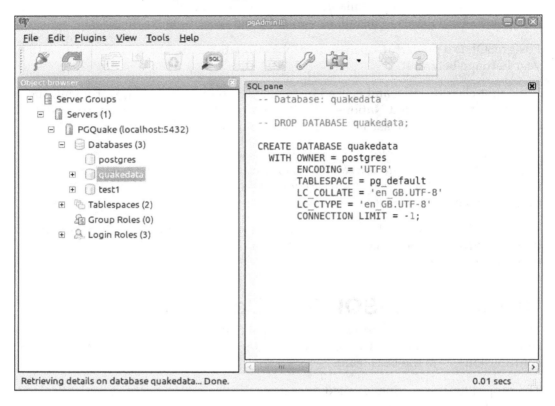

The **File** menu has the option **Add Server...** where a connection to the database server can be made.

Once a connection is available, it can be selected in the tree in the pane on the left. To issue commands to the database, select it from the database list for that server, and choose **Query tool...** from the **Tools** menu.

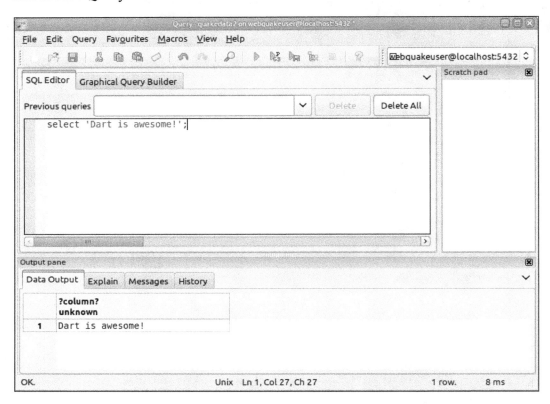

The query tool allows SQL queries to be run against the connected database, and displays the output and results. Enter a query, such as `select 'Dart is awesome!';` and then click on **Execute** in the **Query** menu.

If you prefer, PostgreSQL also has a powerful built-in command line client called `psql`.

Creating the database and login

The database for the application will be called `quakedata`. The login name used will be `webquakeuser` and the password will be `Coco99nut` (case sensitive and without quotes):

```
CREATE DATABASE quakedata
  WITH OWNER = postgres
       ENCODING = 'UTF8'
       TABLESPACE = pg_default
       LC_COLLATE = 'en_GB.UTF-8'
       LC_CTYPE = 'en_GB.UTF-8'
       CONNECTION LIMIT = -1;
```

The SQL script for creating the database is called `CreateDatabase.sql` and can be found in the SQL sub-folder of the sample code for this chapter:

```
CREATE ROLE webquakeuser LOGIN
  ENCRYPTED PASSWORD 'md504a29d543c1492922e76af320cae3190'
  SUPERUSER INHERIT CREATEDB NOCREATEROLE NOREPLICATION;
```

The SQL script for creating the user is called `CreateUser.sql`.

Defining the table

The main table will be a simple storage of the JSON field, with two fields of meta-data, and the SQL to create it can be found in `CreateTable.sql`:

```
CREATE TABLE dm_quakefeed (
    quake_id serial PRIMARY KEY,
    geojson text NOT NULL,
    modified_date TIMESTAMP default CURRENT_TIMESTAMP
    );
```

This SQL defines a table with three fields. The `quake_id` field will be a unique identifier for each record, `geojson` will store the data retrieved from the service, and `modified_date` will record when the insertion into the database was made. Lets have a look at the following screenshot:

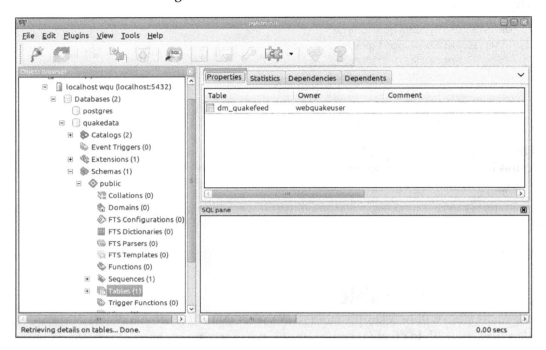

The empty database is now configured and ready to be connected to Dart in order to save the data. The table can be found in the tree in the left-hand side panel **quakedata | Schemas | public | Tables**.

Inserting data

The first step is to create a connection string to connect to the PostgreSQL server. The class `DaoQuake` in `lib/quakedao.dart` handles the database access. This is called by the revised `DataMonitor` class's `fetchData` method, as shown here:

```
if (idPreviousFetch != newId) {
  idPreviousFetch = newId;

  //Save to database.
  await daoGeoJson.storeJson(dataset.toString());

  log.fine("Saved to db $newId - ${dataset.toString()}");
}
```

The `daoGeoJson` instance handles the database interaction. The rest of the data fetching, such as accessing the web service is identical to the file-based version:

```
storeJson(String jsonString) async {
var dbConn;
try {
  dbConn = await connect(uri);
  await dbConn.execute(
      'insert into dm_quakefeed (geojson) values (@geojson)', {
    'geojson': jsonString
  });
} catch (exception, stacktrace) {
  log.severe("Exception storing JSON.", exception, stacktrace);
  print(exception);
  print(stacktrace);
} finally {
  dbConn.close();
}
}
```

The first thing to take note of is that the implementation is wrapped in `try{}`, `catch{}` and `finally{}`. This is because we want a robust solution, even on error conditions. Databases fail and connections fail so the insert may not take place, so we catch exceptions. Once the `dbConn` object is connected to the database server, it runs the SQL statement to store the `jsonString`.

The application needs to manage system resources too, so we always want to close the database connections, which like memory and disk space, are finite resources. The `finally` clause is always executed after the `try`, `catch` and `except` blocks are complete:

```
String uri = 'postgres://webquakeuser:Coco99nut@localhost:5432/
quakedata';
```

The connection to the database is defined in the `uri` connection string, which identifies the server, user name, password, and database. Typically this would be stored in a configuration file.

Running the program

Once the program has been run for a few minutes, data will start to build up in the database. This can be viewed in pgAdmin in the SQL editor, which can be run by clicking the SQL icon on the toolbar:

```
select * from dm_quakefeed;
```

This simple `select` statement will show the table contents:

	geojson text	modified_date date	quake_id integer
1	{type: FeatureCollection, metadata: {generated: 14326618570	2015-05-26	18
2	{type: FeatureCollection, metadata: {generated: 14326619430	2015-05-26	19
3	{type: FeatureCollection, metadata: {generated: 14326619910	2015-05-26	20
4	{type: FeatureCollection, metadata: {generated: 14326620980	2015-05-26	21
5	{type: FeatureCollection, metadata: {generated: 14326621580	2015-05-26	22
6	{type: FeatureCollection, metadata: {generated: 14326621810	2015-05-26	23

Maintaining a database

Setting up a database and writing the accompanying application is only a small part of running a database. Like a garden, they need tending and pruning to get the best results.

We will take a look at writing a maintenance script for the data-monitoring application that will report on the data and clear out the data.

Open the `bin/maintenance.dart` file in the editor.

Managing command line arguments

To switch between these tasks, a command line argument will be used. The Dart `main` function receives a list of Strings as its arguments:

```dart
import 'package:QuakeMonitorDB/quakedao.dart';

main(List<String> arguments) {
  if (arguments.length == 0 || arguments.length > 1) {
    print("Please use either -info or -delete.");
    return 0;
  }

  if (arguments[0] == "-info") {
    var daoGeoJson = new DaoQuake();
    daoGeoJson.displayInfo();
  } else if (arguments[0] == "-delete") {
    var daoGeoJson = new DaoQuake();
    daoGeoJson.deleteRecords();
```

```
    }

    return 0;
}
```

The program skeleton uses the incoming argument to take the appropriate branch.
If too few or two many arguments are passed, a simple message is presented before
ending the program.

Retrieving data

The -info option will return the following data from the database:

Value	Description
Count	Number of records in the table
MinDate	Earliest date
MaxDate	Latest date

The method is implemented in lib/quakedao.dart with a short SQL query to
retrieve the summarized data:

```
displayInfo() async {
  var dbConn;
  try {
    dbConn = await connect(uri);

    var query = """select count(*) as Count,
     min(modified_date) as MinDate,
     max(modified_date) as MaxDate
     from dm_quakefeed
    """;
    var results = await dbConn.query(query).toList();
    print("Count    : ${results[0][0]}");
    print("MinDate : ${results[0][1]}");
    print("MaxDate : ${results[0][2]}");
  } catch (exception, stacktrace) {
    log.severe("Exception getting info.", exception, stacktrace);
    print(exception);
  } finally {
    dbConn.close();
  }
}
```

The result set is returned from PostgreSQL and converted to a list. Each record returned is a list of the column values for that record:

```
Count    : 269
MinDate : 2015-05-26 00:00:00.000
MaxDate : 2015-05-27 00:00:00.000
```

In this instance, we are returned a single record (`result[0]`) containing a list with the three columns (accessed through indices) that contain the information that we need.

Deleting data

This very severe, yet useful, operation is rather simple to implement:

```
deleteRecords() async {
  var dbConn;
  try {
    dbConn = await connect(uri);

    var query = "delete from dm_quakefeed";
    await dbConn.execute(query);
  } catch (exception, stacktrace) {
    log.severe("Exception getting info.", exception, stacktrace);
    print(exception);
  } finally {
    dbConn.close();
  }
}
```

If the maintenance program is re-run with the `-info` option used after this is run, the results are as shown, with `null` meaning that no data is available:

```
Count    : 0
MinDate : null
MaxDate : null
```

Remember to use this very, very carefully!

Observing the Dart VM internals

If you have been watching the output window keenly as you have launched Dart projects, you will have noticed references to the Observatory. This tool (which is part of the Dart SDK) allows developers to look inside a running Dart virtual machine, and profile the ongoing activities. This is useful to find out exactly what an application is doing and where bottlenecks exist.

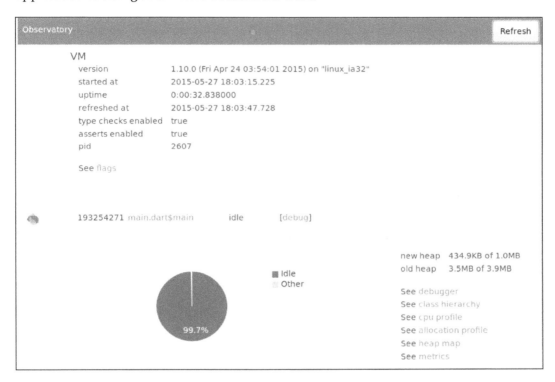

The Observatory supports command line applications and web applications (Dart versions and not the compiled to JavaScript output) running in Dartium. To enable it, simply pass one of the many Observatory command line parameters—see the SDK documents (`https://www.dartlang.org/tools/dart-vm/`) for a full listing:

```
dart --enable-vm-service bin/main.dart
```

Launch the `main.dart` program with the Observatory attached, and browse to the address `localhost:8181` (note that this port number can change though it can be specified in the launch command parameter `--enable-vm-service=<port>/<IP address>`):

```
chromium.exe index.html
```

Launch `index.html` with the Observatory attached. The address to put into the web browser will be shown:

```
Observatory listening on http://127.0.0.1:34935
```

The URLs can be opened in any web browser, the most important feature is the Refresh button, that appears and re-samples the data that is being displayed.

While you are waiting for the data monitor to collect data, take some time to explore the inner workings of the Dart VM as it runs the code.

Unit testing

If you are a Test Driven Development advocate you are probably a bit concerned that we have not written any unit tests so far. That is about to change as we introduce the Dart unit test package, which is simply called `test` (you may see older example code online that uses the older `unittest` package).

In the sample code for this chapter, there is a sub-folder called `Unittest` that contains a unit test in `bin/main.dart`:

```
library Unittestdemo.test;

import 'package:test/test.dart';

void main() {

  test('HelloWorldTest', () {
    expect(1+1, 2);
  });

}
```

This defines a new test called `HelloWorldTest` and the actual test can be carried out by the past in function. The result of the test can be validated using the `expect` method. The library contains an extensive range of matchers to check a result, for example, `isResult`, `isList`, `isNull`, `isTrue` and `isNonPositive`.

Unit Testing focuses on testing a small part of an application at a time. Tests are defined in code, so that they can be run easily and quickly. To ensure they run quickly, true unit tests should not use external resources such as the network or files.

For the code behind an application to be easily unit tested, the design has to allow for the objects to be tested in isolation. For example, all IO may be wrapped into a simple class so that a unit test can be written that uses a fake, or mock, version of the IO class.

This impacts the design but makes sure the code is tested all the way through development. Tests can even be written before the development starts.

Running unit tests

Unit tests are run like any other Dart command line program from your chosen IDE/ Editor or from the command line. For instance, from the Unittest folder the test can be run as dart bin/main.dart:

```
00:00 +0: HelloWorldTest
00:00 +1: All tests passed!
```

The default output for the test runner includes color characters (which may not be supported in your IDE or shell):

```
00:00 +0: HelloWorldTest
00:00 +0 -1: HelloWorldTest
  Expected: <33>
    Actual: <2>

  package:test        expect
  bin/main.dart 9:5   main.<fn>

00:00 +0 -1: Some tests failed.

Unhandled exception:
Uncaught Error: Dummy exception to set exit code.
#0      _rootHandleUncaughtError.<anonymous closure> (dart:async/zone.dart:886)
#1      _asyncRunCallbackLoop (dart:async/schedule_microtask.dart:41)
#2      _asyncRunCallback (dart:async/schedule_microtask.dart:48)
#3      _runPendingImmediateCallback (dart:isolate-patch/isolate_patch.dart:96)
#4      _Timer._runTimers (dart:isolate-patch/timer_impl.dart:392)
#5      _Timer._handleMessage (dart:isolate-patch/timer_impl.dart:411)
```

The output shown gives the names of the test run and the overall result:

```
00:00 +0: HelloWorldTest
00:00 +0 -1: HelloWorldTest
  Expected: <33>
    Actual: <2>

  package:test       expect
  bin/main.dart 9:5  main.<fn>

00:00 +0 -1: Some tests failed.
```

Of course, it doesn't always go well and detail is needed to go and investigate any issue. As well as showing the failing test detail, an exception is thrown so the process running the tests will exit with an error.

Writing unit tests for the data monitor

To get a head start on the next part of the project, we will put together some tests for a class to deal with the contents of the JSON. This is in the `test` folder of the `QuakeMonitorDB` project. The Dart Analyzer will show some issues with these files:

```
Warning: (16, 15) Undefined class 'GeoUpdate'
```

This is because we are writing our tests first, in true **TDD (Test Driven Development)**.

The file `test/qmdb_test.dart` contains the test cases, and `test/data.dart` has some sample data for our tests. Having a fixed set of data is typical for unit testing, as it gives predictable results for the test and does not rely on external resources:

```
test('Object create.', () {
  var o = new GeoUpdate();
  expect(o, isNotNull);
});
```

The first test is a simple creation of the object with no parameters. It is useful to break tests down to this level, as when future changes to the code makes the tests fail, it will be easier to identify at what point the failure occurred.

The sample data for testing is declared as const. What's the difference between final and const? That's a good question!

A final variable is single-assignment and is required to have an initializer. No further changes can be made.

A const object is frozen and completely immutable at compile time.

The keywords final and const provide valuable hints to the compiler about what a variable is, and how it will be used, which can aid performance.

Grouping tests together

It is always good to be organized, and as we may end up with hundreds, if not thousands of unit tests in a large project, they can be grouped together:

```
group('GoodJSON', () {
  var o;
  setUp(() {
    o = new GeoUpdate(sampleJson);
  });
  test('T1. Simple load.', () => expect(o.src, equals(sampleJson)));
  test('T2. Blank load', () {
    o = new GeoUpdate("");
  });
});
```

To run tests, there is sometimes a common set of steps to initialize test objects. The test package provides this facility via the setUp function, which is run before the tests in the group.

There are many more convenient functions and features in the Dart test package, which is constantly being improved. You can follow along and contribute to its development on GitHub.

```
https://github.com/dart-lang/test/
```

The final group of tests focus on Features, which is the name used for the main earthquake entries in the geoJSON feed:

```
group('Features', () {
  var o;
  setUp(() {
```

```
        o = new GeoUpdate(sampleJson);
    });
    test('Test 1', () => expect(o.features.length, equals(5)));
    test('Test 2', () => expect(1, equals(1)));
});
```

Developing tests and the implementation is usually an iterative affair during the development of a project. As the second test in this groups shows, it is easy to put in a placeholder test. Tests help ensure that the final implementation of the code has an upfront design, is loosely coupled, and also provides an easy way to automatically retest a range of functionalities when a change is made.

Contrast running a set of unit tests in a few seconds covering many test cases, taking a few minutes to run a full web application, browsing to a page, entering data, checking the result, and only having covered a single test case.

Examining the test results

Running the unit tests produces results that show all the tests are failing. This is expected as we have not written the implementation yet.

We are not ending the chapter on a low note! What we have done is considered the design, defined some requirements for the object, and created a test suite to validate the solution as we create it.

Summary

Serious applications need robustness, and you will now have a grasp of unit testing in Dart to aid in the rapid production of quality software. We have also covered how to log vital operation details, categorized to the correct level, for long-term monitoring of a system.

Connecting Dart to a serious database is critical for many applications, and you can now carry this out using an industrial-strength database system. You now have the skills to connect to a remote web service to collect real data.

In the next chapter, our exploration of database systems will cover extracting the data into our application, and we will mine this constantly updating data store to populate a rich data grid view of the incoming data, which will be updated in real time.

8
Live Data and a Web Service

Data is a precious thing and will last longer than the systems themselves.

– Tim Berners-Lee

For many today, it is hard to imagine that, at one time, most personal and work computers did not connect to a wider network. Not that long ago, a spontaneous network stream of instant notifications to a device in your pocket was unthinkable.

Newsfeeds, streams, and updates are the standard of web applications today. It is not enough for data to be accessible or discoverable. It has to reach out to the user, ideally even before they know they want it.

Freeing the data

The data that was collected by the data monitor is rather trapped in the database, and while the database system PostgreSQL has a reasonable display in the GUI of pgAdmin, a web page would be more pleasing, and viewable by a wider audience.

Sharing the data to be used by a client? I hope JSON sprung immediately to your mind! The end goal of this phase of the project is a web page that we can visit to view the earthquake information in a friendly manner. The page should update itself smoothly and the data should be made available in a consumable manner for future expansion.

Open the project in the `QuakeMonitorDB` folder in the sample code for this chapter.

Reworking the data collector

The iteration of the GeoJSON data collector in the previous chapter was a straightforward capture of data to the database. In order to make the data easier to handle for other applications, the program will be improved to make a table of individual features listed.

Adding a new data table

The separated features in the database will be stored in a new table named, dm_quakefeatures, as follows:

```
CREATE TABLE dm_quakefeatures
(
  qufeat_id text NOT NULL,
  geojson text NOT NULL,
  modified_date timestamp without time zone DEFAULT now(),
  CONSTRAINT dm_qufeat_pkey PRIMARY KEY (qufeat_id)
)
WITH (
  OIDS=FALSE
);
ALTER TABLE dm_quakefeatures
  OWNER TO webquakeuser;
```

The SQL statements for creating the database are found in the SQL folder of the sample code.

Filtering the data

The DataMonitor class in the file quakemonitordb.dart has an updated fetchData method, which individually stores the underlying features after storing the raw JSON to the database:

```
GeoUpdate update = new GeoUpdate(JSON.encode(dataset));

log.fine("Features to process ${update.features.length}");

for (int i = 0; i < update.features.length; i++) {
  GeoFeature feature = update.features[i];

  await daoGeoJson.storeFeature(feature.id, feature.toJson());
}
```

The GeoUpdate class, which is found in geoupdate.dart, takes a JSON string as a parameter in the constructor. The following excerpt from the constructor shows how it extracts and adds the individual features to the collection:

```
GeoUpdate(String json) {
  src = json;
  features = [];

  if (src.length > 0) {
    try {
      Map rawJsonObj = JSON.decode(src);

      if (rawJsonObj["features"] != null) {
        var items = rawJsonObj["features"];

        items.forEach((Map i) {
          features.add(new GeoFeature(i));
        });
      }
    } catch (exception) {
      print("Error decoding JSON.");
      print("$src");
      print(exception);
    }
  }
}
```

The GeoFeature class, which is found in the geofeature.dart constructor, takes a Map object that is populated with the properties of the feature. The purpose of this is to extract the required information about the feature that needs to be stored for our application, as shown in the following code snippet:

```
GeoFeature(Map newProperties) {
  properties = newProperties["properties"];
  geometry = newProperties["geometry"];
  id = newProperties["id"];
  time = properties["time"].toString();
  title = properties["title"].toString();
  type = properties["type"].toString();
  mag = properties["mag"].toString();
  place = properties["place"].toString();

  url = properties["url"].toString();
  detail = properties["detail"].toString();
}
```

As the preceding excerpt shows, this is not a complicated object that arranges data into convenient fields.

Converting the feature to JSON

To convert the object back to JSON, a specific method will be added, called `toJson`, as shown in the following code snippet:

```
String toJson() {
  Map out = {};
  out["properties"] = properties;
  out["geometry"] = geometry;
  return JSON.encode(out);
}
```

The key fields of `properties` and `geometry` are added to `Map` before being passed to the encoding function and returned to the caller.

Improving the data maintenance

Since there is a new table in the database, we will want to update the maintenance program `maintenance.dart` to clear both tables, as shown in the following code snippet:

```
deleteRecords() async {
  var dbConn;
  try {
    dbConn = await connect(uri);

    var query = "delete from dm_quakefeed";
    await dbConn.execute(query);

    query = "delete from dm_quakefeatures";
    await dbConn.execute(query);
  } catch (exception, stacktrace) {
    log.severe("Exception getting info.", exception, stacktrace);
    print(exception);
  } finally {
    dbConn.close();
  }
}
```

This is carried out by using another `delete` SQL statement, and reuses the existing connection to the database.

Storing the single feature

The storage of the feature will take two separate queries. The first will use the ID field to check if it is currently in the table. If it is, then the function will exit without storing the JSON string. Let's have a look at the following code snippet:

```
storeFeature(String featureID, String json) async {
  var dbConn;
  try {
    dbConn = await connect(uri);

    var query = """select count(*) as Count
      from dm_quakefeatures where qufeat_id ='$featureID'
    """;
    var results = await dbConn.query(query).toList();

    if (results[0][0] != 0) return;

    await dbConn.execute(
        'insert into dm_quakefeatures (qufeat_id, geojson) values (@
qufeat_id, @geojson)',
        {'qufeat_id': featureID, 'geojson': json});
  } catch (exception, stacktrace) {
    log.severe("Exception storing Feature.", exception, stacktrace);
    print(exception);
    print(stacktrace);
  } finally {
    dbConn.close();
  }
}
```

The first query returns the number of records that match the ID. The result returned is converted to a list format, and the value is accessed via `[0][0]` — the first record and first field. If the result is not zero, then the method returns without further action.

The second SQL operation stores the feature in the database by using an `insert` statement.

Running the data application

The application can be run as usual from the command line. You may wish to run the data collector like this in order to save having multiple IDEs open for a long period of time. Let's have a look at the following code snippet:

```
$ cd QuakeMonitorDB/
QuakeMonitorDB$ dart bin/main.dart
Starting QuakeMonitor DB version...
```

This shows the launching of the QuakeMonitor program in a terminal. If a close look is taken at the processes running on the system, the resources used by the Dart VM can be seen, as shown in the following screenshot:

```
Tasks: 143 total,   1 running, 142 sleeping,   0 stopped,   0 zombie
%Cpu(s): 20.5 us,   5.5 sy,  0.0 ni, 41.6 id, 32.4 wa,  0.0 hi,  0.0 si,  0.0 st
KiB Mem:   2063184 total,  1891244 used,   171940 free,   175320 buffers
KiB Swap:  1047548 total,     3048 used,  1044500 free.   872680 cached Mem

  PID USER      PR  NI    VIRT    RES    SHR S %CPU %MEM     TIME+ COMMAND
 1587 daftspa+  20   0  446328 105652  43228 S 15.6  5.1   1:10.49 dropbox
 1025 root      20   0  175268  52076  33536 S  3.6  2.5   1:07.62 Xorg
 1651 daftspa+  20   0  144992  27252  21508 S  2.7  1.3   0:01.47 mate-terminal
 2546 daftspa+  20   0   65960  24984   8764 S  1.7  1.2   0:04.36 dart
 1911 daftspa+  20   0  147900 127324   8544 S  1.3  6.2   0:41.80 dart
 1748 daftspa+  20   0 1073912 290220  23496 S  0.7 14.1   1:50.81 java
 2403 root      20   0       0      0      0 S  0.7  0.0   0:03.64 kworker/0:1
    7 root      20   0       0      0      0 S  0.3  0.0   0:01.99 rcu_sched
```

The Dart process launched for the QuakeMonitor measures approximately a mere 64 megabytes, and starts nearly instantly.

Creating the web service

Now that the data collection and storage has been re-factored, it is time to build a web service. In some ways, this is similar to the blog server we created previously. However, we want to be ambitious, and so will plan for future development by starting to build a web API for our data.

The REST architecture style is very popular as it is well suited to JSON and being consumed by client web applications.

REST is an architecture style for web services that has gained acceptance as a less complex alternative to WSDL and SOAP.

REST builds on HTTP and uses the verbs GET, POST, PUT, and DELETE. It can use any Internet format as a data type (XML, images, and so on), but usually uses JSON.

There is no agreed standard for RESTful web APIs, as it is a style rather than a protocol. This means that it is very flexible, but it can also be hard to get an answer to questions such as "is this the right way to do it?". The usual advice is to be pragmatic and follow REST as far as makes sense.

For more information, see http://www.restapitutorial.com/.

Using the package rpc

A RESTful API has a number of conventions and expectations. Fortunately, there is an existing Dart package, authored by the Dart development team, that covers most of the implementation detail.

The rpc package is available from Pub at https://pub.dartlang.org/packages/rpc.

The source code is available from GitHub at https://github.com/dart-lang/rpc.

As a bonus, the rpc package also includes discoverability features (via Google's Discovery Document, https://developers.google.com/discovery/v1/reference/apis), which allow the easy creation of client code in any supporting language.

Initiating the API server

In the main.dart file, the server is set up and set to serve on the local machine using port 8080, as shown in the following code snippet:

```
library io_rpc_sample;

import 'dart:io';
import 'package:georestwebservice/georestwebservice.dart';
import 'package:rpc/rpc.dart';

final ApiServer _apiServer = new ApiServer(apiPrefix: '/api',
prettyPrint: true);
```

```
main() async {
  _apiServer.addApi(new Quake());
  _apiServer.enableDiscoveryApi();

  HttpServer server = await HttpServer.bind(InternetAddress.ANY_IP_V4,
8080);
  server.listen(_apiServer.httpRequestHandler);
}
```

The _apiServer instance is set up with two parameters. The first sets an expected prefix for the API so that valid URLs will start with the form http://127.0.0.1:8080/api. The second parameter, prettyPrint, formats the JSON for easy viewing in the browser or another consuming application that may include a debugger. This is particularly useful when the JSON is heavily nested.

The _apiServer instance is then configured with a Quake object. This object contains the implementation of the API methods. The Quake class definition is located in the file georestwebservice.dart, and is heavily annotated. Let's have a look at the following code snippet:

```
@ApiClass(
    name: 'quake',
    version: 'v1',
    description: 'Rest API for Earthquake feature data.')
class Quake {
  ...
}
```

The @ApiClass annotation exposes this class as an API on the rpc server. This allows separate class to handle the implementation per API name and per version. The different versions are accessed by changing the version or name in the URL that is being requested from the server.

Exposing methods

The simplest method is the classic Hello World example:

```
@ApiMethod(path: 'hello')
QuakeResponse hello() {
  return new QuakeResponse()..result = 'Hello world.';
}
```

The `path` setting in the attribute defines the name part of the URL. A `QuakeResponse` object is returned with a string set as the result, as shown in the following screenshot:

The `QuakeResponse` class is a simple class that is automatically converted to a JSON response by the `rpc` package, as shown in the following code snippet:

```
class QuakeResponse {
  String result;
  QuakeResponse();
}
```

Classes used as a response are required to be concrete (not abstract) and to have a constructor with no parameters. Also, the constructor must not be a named constructor.

Error handling of incorrect requests

The `rpc` package handles any URLs for incorrect methods automatically, and provides an error message in JSON format:

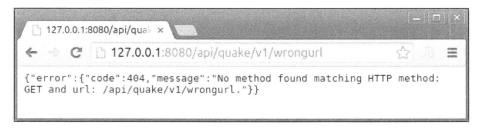

The error handling also covers an exception or other error occurring within the implementation of an API method, as shown here:

```
@ApiMethod(path: 'implementationerror')
QuakeResponse implementationError() {
  throw new Exception();
}
```

This doomed-to-fail method will produce a valid JSON response that the client application can handle:

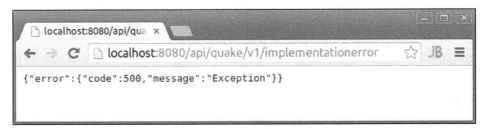

Serving the latest information

For the grid view data display, the most important URL for the web API will be `http://127.0.0.1:8080/api/quake/v1/latest`:

```
@ApiMethod(path: 'latest')
List<String> latest()  {
  DaoQuakeAPI qa = new DaoQuakeAPI();
  return qa.fetchTopTenLatest();
}
```

The `rpc` package handles the conversion to JSON of several common return types. The `List<String>` is probably the most common collection.

Supplying the data

The `DaoQuakeAPI` class is implemented in the file `daoapi.dart` and retrieves the features list from the database, as shown in the following code snippet:

```
Future<List<String>> fetchTopTenLatest() async {
  var dbConn;
  try {
    dbConn = await connect(uri);

    var query = """
    select geojson from dm_quakefeatures order by modified_date desc
limit 10
    """;

    List<Row> dbResults = await dbConn.query(query).toList();
    List<String> results = new List<String>();
```

```
    dbResults.forEach((record) {
      results.add(record[0]);
    });

    return results;
  } catch (exception, stackTrace) {
    print(exception);
    print(stackTrace);
  } finally {
    dbConn.close();
  }
}
```

The results are returned as a list of records, and each record returned is a `List` object. This means that `dbr[0]` needs to be specified, as we only require the string in the first field.

Discovering the API

The `rpc` package provides built-in discoverability for the API. This is provided as a JSON definition of the service that is accessed from the API server:

```
http://127.0.0.1:8080/api/discovery/v1/apis/quake/v1/rest
```

This definition would be consumed by development tools to produce wrapper objects and supporting code in the required language. Let's have a look at the output in the following screenshot:

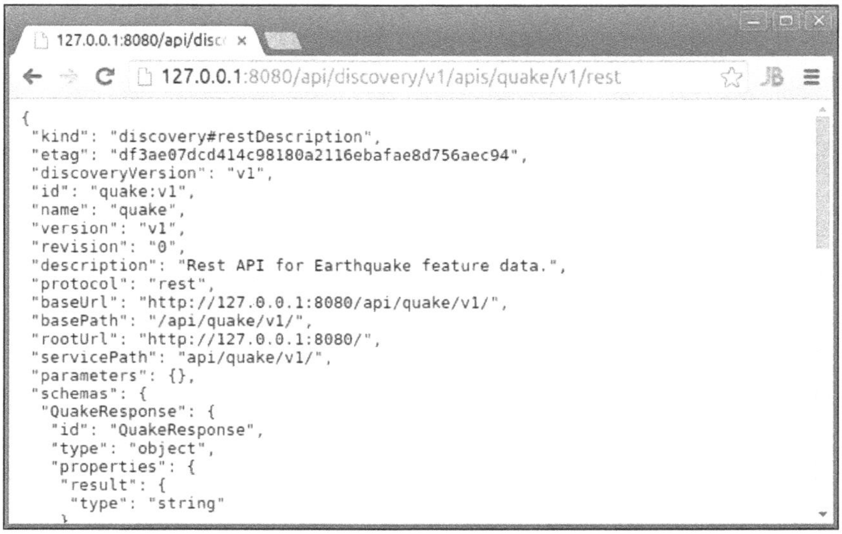

The header contains identifying information, like the version, and key usage data, such as the base URL for calling methods.

The `schemas` section summarizes all the data types used by the API, the methods lists, and the available function calls that can be made. In addition, the resources section (empty for this project) would contain the objects that group API methods together.

Running the web service

As with the data monitor, you may wish to run the REST web service outside of the development environment. To run from a terminal (command line), enter the following code:

```
$ cd georestwebservice/
$ dart bin/main.dart
Starting georestwebservice...
```

Recapping the system so far

We now have two parts of the system in place. The first contacts the live feed and pulls out the breaking information, and the second exposes the collected data via a standard API:

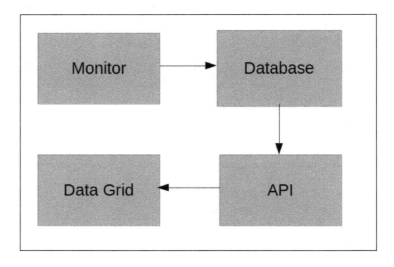

Both of these will need to be running, and it would be advisable to have them running outside the development environment. This varies between operating systems, so use a batch file or shell script as appropriate.

Open a process explorer application (`top` on the Linux command line, Task Manager on Windows, or Activity Monitor on Mac OS) and you will be able to see how efficient the Dart VM is. The applications start immediately and use a relatively small amount of memory.

Consuming application

We now have two parts of the solution: the collected data and the web service to publish it. The next step is to build a client application that will talk to the web service. Initially, we will have a details grid view (or `table` for the HTML-minded) of the ten latest incoming data.

Rather than having the user update the page, the screen will auto-update periodically with the latest earthquake information.

Packaging the grid

The grid display may be useful for other applications, so it will be split off into its own project as the package `webgridview`, as shown here:

```
name: 'GridViewer'
version: 0.0.1
description: A grid viewer for GeoJSON data.
environment:
  sdk: '>=1.0.0 <2.0.0'
dependencies:
  browser: '>=0.10.0 <0.11.0'
  intl: any
  webgridview:
    path: ../webgridview/
```

The package can be referenced in the `pubspec.yaml` as a local package.

Initiating the real-time updates

The `main` function in `main.dart` will perform an initial update of the grid and then initiate a `Timer` that will update the page on a periodic basis:

```
void main() {
  performUpdate(null);
  updater = new Timer.periodic(new Duration(seconds: 10),
performUpdate);
}
```

The periodic timer handler `performUpdate` is provided a `Timer` object as a parameter when it is triggered every *10* seconds. When we are directly calling it, `null` is provided instead of the `Timer` instance.

Performing the update

The two elements being updated are the current time, with a countdown to the next refresh, and the grid of the data. Let's have a look at the following code snippet:

```
void performUpdate(Timer triggerTimer) {
  DivElement outputDiv = querySelector('#timestatus');

  DateTime currentDateTime = new DateTime.now();
  DateFormat timeStamp = new DateFormat("hh:mm a");

  if (triggerTimer != null) {
    secondsToUpdate -= 10;
  } else updateDataView();

  if (secondsToUpdate == 0) {
    updateDataView();
    secondsToUpdate = 60;
  }

  outputDiv.text =
      "${timeStamp.format(currentDateTime)} - $secondsToUpdate seconds
until refresh.";
}
```

The `secondsToUpdate` variable is decremented from `60` to `0` and triggers an update every *six* calls so that the display changes every minute.

Fetching the JSON

The `updateDataView` function in the `main.dart` file covers fetching the data and updating the grid view:

```
...

HttpRequest.getString(jsonSrc).then((String data) {
  outputDiv.children.clear();

  List items;
  try {
```

```
    items = JSON.decode(data);
  } catch (exception, stackTrace) {
    print(exception);
    print(stackTrace);
  }
...
```

The `DivElement` `outputDiv` is the container for the dynamically updating content, which is entirely cleared at each update. The incoming JSON data is decoded and stored in the `List` object named `items`.

Configuring the grid view control

The data for the grid is provided as a structure of a list of lists. The first list in the structure forms the header of the table. Let's have a look at the following code snippet:

```
...
if (items != null) {
  List allQuakeData = [];
  allQuakeData.add(
      ['Time', 'Magnitude', 'Type', 'Tsunami', 'Place', 'Sig',
'Link']);

  items.forEach((String post) {
    Map decodedData = JSON.decode(post);

    List quakeData = [];
    quakeData.add(convertTime(decodedData['properties']['time']));
    quakeData.add(decodedData['properties']['mag']);
    quakeData.add(decodedData['properties']['type']);
    quakeData.add(decodedData['properties']['tsunami']);
    quakeData.add(decodedData['properties']['place']);
    quakeData.add(decodedData['properties']['sig']);
    quakeData.add(decodedData['properties']['url']);

    allQuakeData.add(quakeData);
  });

  outputDiv.append(Gridview.getTable(allQuakeData));
}
...
```

The JSON items are iterated over and the values for the grid are extracted. The only value not used directly is the `time` field, which requires formatting.

Formatting the time

The time provided for each feature in the JSON is an integer number. This is the time recorded as the number of milliseconds since a point in time, usually called the epoch (which is the start of the year *1970* at exactly *00:00:00 1970-01-01*). Let's have a look at the following code snippet:

```
String convertTime(int milliTime) {
  DateTime dt = new DateTime.fromMillisecondsSinceEpoch(milliTime);
  DateFormat timeStamp = new DateFormat("hh:mm:ss a");
  return timeStamp.format(dt);
}
```

The `DateTime` format provides the named constructor `fromMillisecondsSinceEpoch`, which returns a regular `DateTime` object. This can be converted to a string and added to the table for display in the data grid.

Working with date and time

Dates and times are very important data types in all kinds of applications, and the Dart `intl` package has functionality for parsing and formatting dates. Countries have specific formatting and ordering preferences, and, of course, everyone is different and uses multiple formats.

The format used in the grid view may not be to your liking and may be better displayed as a 24-hour format. The project `timesdate` in the sample code for this chapter explores the different date formats that are available. This short command-line program shows some of the options available; the list is quite long, and it is fully documented in the `intl` package documentation. Let's have a look at the following code snippet:

```
DateTime currentTime = new DateTime.now();

print("\nDate and Time Demo");
printTime(currentTime, "hh:mm a");
printTime(currentTime, "HH:MM");
printTime(currentTime, "y");
printTime(currentTime, "d");
printTime(currentTime, "M");
printTime(currentTime, "EEEE");
...
```

The preceding code renders the following output display, which will vary according to the time at which it is executed:

```
Date and Time Demo
hh:mm a      04:12 PM
HH:MM        16:06
y            2015
d            13
EEEE         Saturday
```

The function `printTime` formats the input `DateTime` to the desired style. The `padRight` method on the `String` object is used to make a simple table by adding spaces to pad out the string to 12 characters, as shown here:

```
void printTime(DateTime dt, String format) {
    DateFormat timeStamp = new DateFormat(format);
    print("\t${format.padRight(12)} ${timeStamp.format(dt)}");
}
```

The second part of the program allows a date to be entered by using the `stdin` `readlineSync` method. The user can enter a blank line to exit. The string is parsed according to the format `yyyy-MM-dd`, and the weekday is displayed if it is successfully parsed:

```
while (true) {
  String userDate = "";
  print("\nPlease enter a date (yyyy-MM-dd):");

  try {
    DateFormat timeStamp = new DateFormat("yyyy-MM-dd");
    DateFormat outputFmt = new DateFormat("EEEE");

    userDate = stdin.readLineSync();
    if (userDate.length == 0) exit(0);

    print(outputFmt.format(timeStamp.parse(userDate)));
  } catch (exception, stacktrace) {
    print('Error parsing the entered date.');
    print(exception);
    print(stacktrace);
  }
}
```

The parsing is wrapped in `try catch` to deal with an exception raise with a failed parse of a date string.

Building the table

The class `GridView`, located in the file `lib/src/webgridview_base.dart`, prepares a table from the list of lists provided by the calling web page. The static method `getTable` performs the task. As it is static, an instance of the class is not required to call this function. Let's have a look at the following code snippet:

```
static TableElement getTable(List rows) {
  TableElement te = new TableElement();
  rows.forEach((row) => addRow(te, row));
  return te;
}
```

The `addRow` function iterates over the columns in the results. The header row is added as a regular row as the CSS will take care of the special formatting of the first row, as shown here:

```
static addRow(TableElement table, List cols) {
TableRowElement tableRow = table.addRow();

cols.forEach((column) {
  TableCellElement tableCell = tableRow.addCell();
  String content = column.toString();
  if (content.startsWith('http')) {
    content = "<a href=\"$content\">Link</a>";
    tableCell.appendHtml(content);
  } else tableCell.text = content;
});
}
```

The content is added as text to the table cell, with one special case of strings that start with `http`. These URLs are formatted into HTML with a generic link text, and the `appendHtml` method is used to ensure that the text is not sanitized before being added to the page.

Showing the page

Launching the application in Dartium will show the `index.html` page:

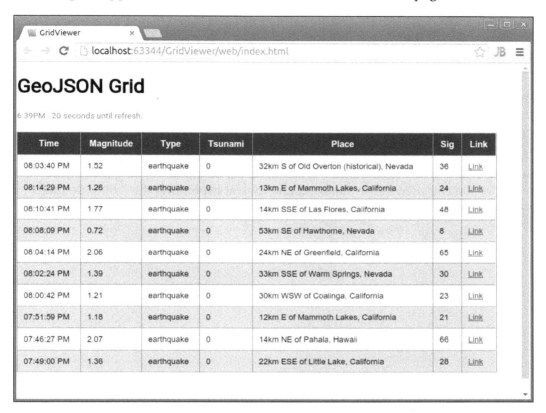

Keep this page open over a period of time and the table will update smoothly as new data becomes available. Events from outside the USA do appear, though less often. It is fairly rare, but the Type column does not always read 'earthquake'.

Summary

The applications created in this chapter have been numerous, but all work together to reach the goal of a live display of data.

The data collector transforms raw live data into a processable form. The REST API was created with the `rpc` package, taking much of the work out of the way. Creating a new web API method is a case of adding an annotated regular Dart method.

The consuming web application showed how to connect to a JSON standard web service and produce high-quality output, updated in real time. The HTML DOM was used to swap in a new table-based display.

The incoming data on earthquakes has proven quite fascinating to watch, but it could be more visual. In the next chapter, we'll create a visualization using the feature geometry data stashed in the database, and look at expanding the API to do more than provide a data feed.

A Real-Time Visualization

There's just something hypnotic about maps.

– Ken Jennings

Maps are indeed hypnotic as are flashing indicator lights, which may give you a rough idea of where the earthquake monitor project is going next. It is the logical format to display all that rich geographical data we are collecting.

An animated display is one step up from a static display, and the step beyond animation is to make it interactive. We will look at accessing the web browser features from Dart in order to integrate to the desktop and work with the user's location.

To work in a professional development environment or to share with the community online, we will need to create documentation from our Dart source.

Iteration overview

The grid view gave a very detailed view of the data obtained from the stack of software that collected the data from the web service, was stored in a database, and was then shared from the database via an API.

For this part of the project, we will reuse every part other than a `gridview`, and build a new visualization using a world map.

Let's take a look at how the map view fits into the overall system:

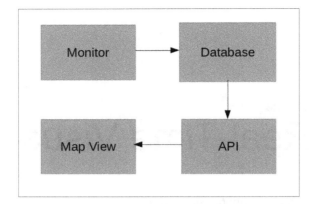

To ensure the map view has some data, the **Monitor** needs to be running, as does the API.

The main project for this chapter is the mapviewer project in the sample code bundle.

Application overview

The mapviewer project is a Dart web application with an index.html entry point that kicks off the application on main.dart:

```
main() async {
  quakeMap = new MapDisplay(querySelector('#mapview'), width, height);
  await quakeMap.loadImage();

  featPlotter = new FeaturePlotter(width, height, quakeMap.mapCtx);

  quakeMap.showPopup = showPopup;
  quakeUpdate();

  querySelector('#zoombtn').onClick.listen(zoomMap);
  querySelector('#locatebtn').onClick.listen(locateUser);
  querySelector('#sortbtn').onClick.listen(sortFeatures);

  new Timer.periodic(new Duration(seconds: 60), quakeUpdate);
  new Timer.periodic(new Duration(milliseconds: 100),
animationUpdate);
}
```

The `MapDisplay` class sets up the map on the web page (on the `div` element with the ID `mapview`) and the image is loaded in. Then, `quakeUpdate()` is called to ensure the initial display of the map and data on the page.

Once the initial display is handled, the **Zoom** button is connected to the `zoomMap` function. Then the two timers have handlers to deal with updating the quake data and the animation display. The `FeaturePlotter` class handles the data and display updates and is used by `quakeUpdate` and `animationUpdate`.

Drawing the map image

The HTML5 canvas will host the live display. The background is a block-like map of the world; feel free to find and use a different version!

Let's have a look at the following screenshot:

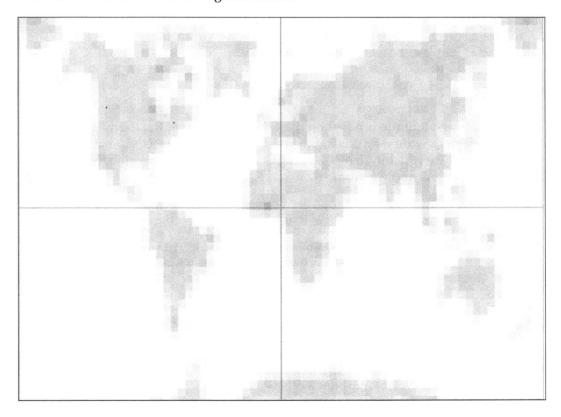

The red lines represent *0* degrees of latitude and longitude.

Plotting on the map

The geometry point contains three pieces of data in a list called `coordinates`. They are the **longitude, latitude,** and also the **depth** in kilometers of where the earthquake originated:

```
{type: Point, coordinates: [-117.4505005, 34.2316666, 13.31]}
```

To map these coordinates to the map, we use the method `toPoint` in the `FeaturePlotter` class in the file `featureplotter.dart`, which performs the conversion as follows:

```
Point toPoint(double longitude, double latitude) {
  double x = 0.0;
  double y = 0.0;
  double hdeg = width.toDouble() / 360;
  double vdeg = height.toDouble() / 180;

  x = (width / 2) + (hdeg * longitude);
  y = (height / 2) - (vdeg * latitude);

  return new Point(x.toInt(), y.toInt());
}
```

The longitude and latitude is based on the spherical nature of the Earth, and the x axis is 360 degrees wide with 0 being the mid-point. The y axis is 180 with 0 being the midpoint at the equator. In terms of the GeoJSON data, the x values are in the range of 180 to +180 and y is from -90 to 90.

Dart, at the time of writing is at version 1.11 and you may be wondering if it will reach version 2 in the near future. Yes, it will!

During the first Dart Developer Summit, version 2 of Dart was mentioned for the first time by Lars Bak. While it was hinted that there may be some language changes, it was strongly emphasized these would only be made with tools to handle updating existing code. In Bak's words, "this is not Python!" This quote is a reference for the somewhat disruptive move from Python 2 to Python 3.

One key change that has already begun is the moving of some packages out of the SDK. This allows them to update on their own schedule. For example, `dart:html` has to respond more quickly than the SDK update cycle to web browser changes.

Animating the display

The `animationUpdate` handler set up in the `main` function in the `main.dart` file fires the `FeaturePlotter` method `updateDisplay`:

```
void animationUpdate([Timer t = null]) {
  featPlotter.updateDisplay();
}
```

This method in turn calls an update on each map indicator object instance, as shown in the following code snippet. The `userLocation` will be covered later in this chapter:

```
void updateDisplay() {
  mapIndicators.forEach((mapIndicator) => mapIndicator.update());
  userLocation.forEach((mapIndicator) => mapIndicator.update());
}
```

The `MapIndicator` class in `mapindicator.dart` handles the display and animation of the feature. The display will be a growing circle point with the maximum size of the point matching the magnitude of the earthquake event. The constructor and update method handle the task of keeping the plotted shape within range:

```
MapIndicator(this.x, this.y, this.ctx, this.magnitude) {
  maxWidth = (width + 1) + magnitude * 2;
}

void update() {
  width++;
  if (width == maxWidth) width = 0;
  draw();
}
```

This will cause the point width to grow upwards to the limit before being reset back to a value of 0, as shown here:

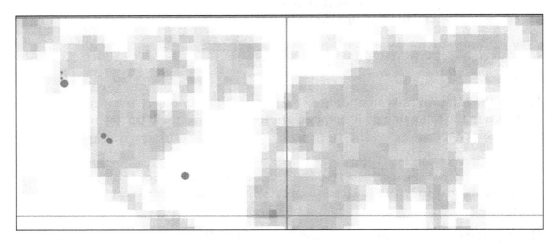

The circle is drawn using the arc method of the HTML5 canvas:

```
void draw() {
  ctx
    ..beginPath()
    ..arc(x, y, width, 0, 2 * PI, false)
    ..fillStyle = colorPrimary
    ..fill()
    ..lineWidth = 1
    ..strokeStyle = colorSecondary
    ..stroke();
}
```

The x and y specify the point where the feature will be drawn and w specifies the radius. The next two parameters are the start and end angles, which are measured in radians, and in a circle there are 2 * PI radians. The constant value for PI is taken from the dart:math library, which is amongst the imports of this class. The last parameter of this method is a flag to determine whether the arc should be drawn counterclockwise or not.

Fetching the data

The data is fetched as an HttpRequest in the same manner as in the grid view project, and the fields we are interested in are put into the list quakepoints before being filtered into the geoFeatures list:

```
fetchFeatureList() async {
  geoFeatures.clear();

  String data = await HttpRequest.getString(jsonSrc);
  List items;
  List quakePoints = [];

  try {
    items = JSON.decode(data);
  } catch (exception, stacktrace) {
    print(exception);
    print(stacktrace);
  }

  if (items != null) {
    items.forEach((String post) {
      Map feature = JSON.decode(post);

      List quakedata = [
        feature['geometry']['coordinates'][0],
        feature['geometry']['coordinates'][1],
        feature['properties']['mag'],
        feature['properties']['place'],
        feature['properties']['type'],
        feature['geometry']['coordinates'][2]
      ];

      quakePoints.add(quakedata);
    });

    quakePoints.where((qp) => qp[4] == 'earthquake').forEach((qp) {
      geoFeatures.add(qp);
    });
  }
}
```

All the items returned are added to the quake points list, but we only want to add the earthquake ones to the geoFeatures list. The list may contain other types such as quarry blast.

Using a where clause, we can filter the list an item at a time. The list item is run through the function, and the list item at index number 4 is compared against the string earthquake.

This is a very convenient method for getting only the required data and best of all it is available on any iterable object. On top of this, there are number of variants such as firstWhere and lastWhere that help to quickly get a reference to the data that matches a criterion.

Updating the map indicators

Once a list of geoFeatures is available, it can be used to construct a list of mapIndicator objects that will appear on the map. The entire list is cleared out each time so that the number of indicators on the map does not build up too much over time. Let's take a look at the following screenshot:

```
updateData() async {
  await fetchFeatureList();
  mapIndicators.clear();
  geoFeatures.forEach((List feature) {
    Point pos = toPoint(feature[0], feature[1]);
    MapIndicator mi;
    mi = new MapIndicator(pos.x, pos.y, ctx, feature[2].toInt());
    mi.summary = "Magnitude ${feature[2]} - ${feature[3]}.";
    mapIndicators.add(mi);
  });
}
```

This function is marked async as there is an await being used for the fetchFeatureList method call. Once the features are available, the mapIndicators list is reset and a new one is constructed.

Mouse over popups

To give the user more details about the feature on the map, a popup appears at the top of the screen when the pointer is moved over a map indicator. To get the mouse pointer coordinates, a handler can be added to handle the mouse move events on the canvas element:

```
MapDisplay(CanvasElement mapcanvas, this.width, this.height) {
  mapctx = mapcanvas.getContext("2d");
  mapcanvas.onMouseMove.listen(mouseMove);
}
```

This is carried out in the MapDisplay constructor and the method handles the triggering of the implementation function. This function is a field in the class that is set by the page using the map display:

```
void mouseMove(MouseEvent e) {
  if (showPopup != null)
    showPopup(e.client.x - 50, e.client.y - 90);
}
```

The implementation of the showPopup function is in main.dart. It displays the initially hidden popup above the map and then populates it with the feature details:

```
void showPopup(int x, int y) {
  bool inHotspot = false;

  if (zoomed) {
    x = x ~/ 2;
    y = y ~/ 2;
  }

  featPlotter.hotspotInfo.forEach((Rectangle<int> key, String value) {
    if (key.containsPoint(new Point(x, y))) {
      inHotspot = true;
      querySelector('#popup').innerHtml = value;
    }
  });

  if (inHotspot)
    querySelector('#popup').style.visibility = "visible";
}
```

If the map display is zoomed in, then the coordinates must be updated; this is performed with the `~/` division operator, which returns an integer value. This is faster than the equivalent `(x/2).toInt()` and gives the required whole numbers for plotting:

4.8 - 50km WSW of Purac, Philippines.

The `Map` containing the `hotspotInfo` is iterated over with a convenient `forEach` loop, giving both the dictionary `key` and the respective `value`. The current point of the mouse relative to the top-left corner of the canvas element is tested against each rectangle that defines the hotspot (the hotspot is the area on the map that will trigger the popup).

The hotspots are stored as a list of `Rectangle<int>` objects generated when the data list is being updated by the `FeaturePlotter` class. This class is from the `dart:math` package:

```
void updateHotspots() {
  hotspotInfo.clear();
  mapIndicators.forEach((MapIndicator mi) {
    Rectangle<int> rect = new Rectangle(mi.x - mi.maxWidth,
        mi.y - mi.maxWidth, mi.maxWidth * 2, mi.maxWidth * 2);

    hotspotInfo[rect] = mi.summary;
  });
}
```

The hotspot is defined as a square area around the map indicator when it is at its maximum width. The `summary` property gives the text to be displayed. The screenshot of the quake map is as follows:

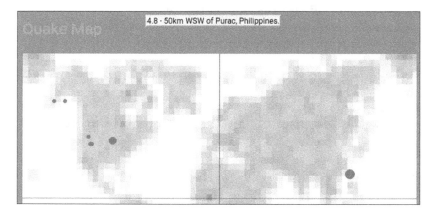

Hopefully, this can help you in improving your geographical knowledge and learning more about Dart!

When debugging in Dartium using a REST or other similar web service, it is possible to get extra logging in the console window of the browser's developer tools for XMLHTTPrequests.

Bring up the context menu (right-click), and there is an option named **Log XMLHttpRequests** that displays the HTTP requests made by the web page in the console output window:

```
[-121.5371704, 36.8165016, 0.93]
129.91739911111114 177.278328
2.2222222222222223 3.3333333333333335
maxWidth 2
XHR finished loading: GET "http://127.0.0.1:8080/api/
quake/v1/latest".
```

This can be invaluable when debugging a project and saves adding logging to every part of the code that makes an HTTP request.

Zooming into the display

The canvas element has a range of features for 2D drawing, and this includes a scaling feature that we can use to hone in on the most active part of the map, North America. In main.dart, a flag exists called zoomed, defaulting to false, that aids the application in keeping track of the current display. A button is bound to the zoom code implementation:

```
zoomMap(Event evt) async {
  if (zoomed == true) {
    zoomed = false;
    quakeMap.mapCtx.resetTransform();
    quakeMap.mapCtx.scale(1, 1);
  } else {
    zoomed = true;
    quakeMap.mapCtx.scale(2, 2);
  }
  quakeMap.drawMapGrid();
}
```

The canvas is toggled between scaling settings, with a critical call to the method `resetTransfom`. Without this, the scaling would not be back to normal. The entire map view must be redrawn immediately so that the user has a responsive experience. Let's have a look at the following screenshot:

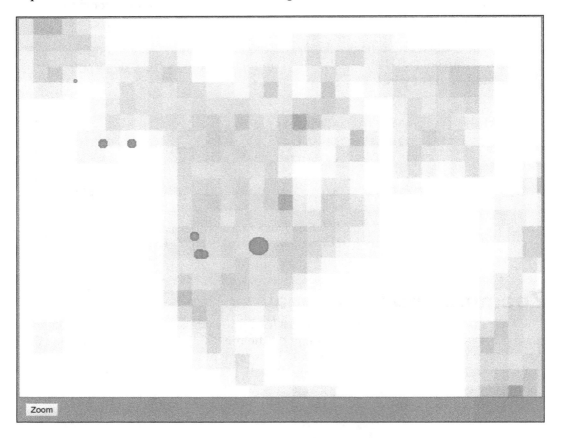

If you watch this page for a while, you will find the California and Alaska feature embedded heavily in the data. As the pop-up code handles the change in scale, these are still available. Pressing the **Zoom** button a second time returns to the full world view.

> The `print` function is not just for command-line applications but can be used in web applications, too. The output appears in the **Developer Tools** console log window, which can be displayed by right-clicking on the page to bring up the context menu and then clicking `Inspect Element`.

Notifying the user of an update

However impressive a created display is it is unlikely to hold the user's attention forever and they are likely to switch to another application or browser tab. Luckily, HTML5 has a feature that will allow notifications on the desktop.

The `main.dart` function `quakeUpdate` checks if there is a significant update to notify the user about. To determine which item in the list to notify the user about, the `lastWhere` method is used. This `List` method finds the last item in the list that matches the criteria defined by the supplied function. In this case, we look at each feature's magnitude value (stored in `gf[2]`) and return `true` or `false` if the value meets the threshold:

```dart
quakeUpdate([Timer t = null]) async {
  await featPlotter.updateData();
  featPlotter.updateHotspots();
  quakeMap.drawMapGrid();

  List notiFeature =
      featPlotter.geoFeatures.lastWhere((List gf) => gf[2] > 1.9);

  String permResult = await Notification.requestPermission();
  if (permResult == 'granted') {
    Notification notifyQuake = new Notification('Quake Alert',
        body: 'Quake Update ${notiFeature[3]} - ${notiFeature[2]}');
  }
}
```

As this feature is potentially intrusive to a user's computer, the web page must ask for permission to show alerts. In Dartium, a prompt is shown at the top of the page requiring a yes or no response:

Once permission has been granted, the final step is to create an instance of the notification class. No further method call is required:

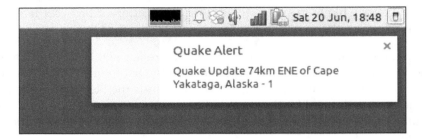

The application is set to notify quite often—you may wish to raise the level at which quakes are notified or you will find yourself dismissing a lot of notifications. The visual display of the notification may vary on different platforms and web browsers.

Plotting the user's location

Most mobile devices are fitted with a geolocation device, or the location can be determined using secondary information such as IP or even falling back to user input. This is exposed for the modern web developer to use in applications via the HTML5 geolocation API at `http://www.w3.org/TR/geolocation-API/`.

As with the desktop notifications, the user must give permission for the page to use their location. A further little hurdle is that location features do not work on Dartium. To try out this feature of the application, use `pub build` to create the JavaScript version and use another browser:

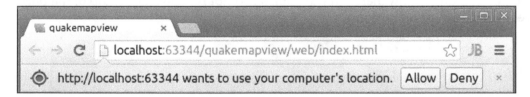

The **Locate** button on the page will attempt to obtain the user's position and draw it on the page by adding it to the `featurePlotter` class instance:

```
locateUser(Event evt) async {
  Geoposition geoPos = await window.navigator.geolocation.
getCurrentPosition();
  MapIndicator mapIndicator;
  var pos =
```

```
        featPlotter.toPoint(geoPos.coords.longitude, geoPos.coords.
latitude);
    mapIndicator = new MapIndicator(pos.x, pos.y, quakeMap.mapCtx, 4);
    mapIndicator.colorPrimary = "#0000ff";
    mapIndicator.colorSecondary = "#00ffff";
    featPlotter.userLocation.add(mapIndicator);
}
```

The coordinates are converted in the same manner as the quakes, and the indicator is changed to a blue color so that it will stand out on the map, as shown in the following screenshot:

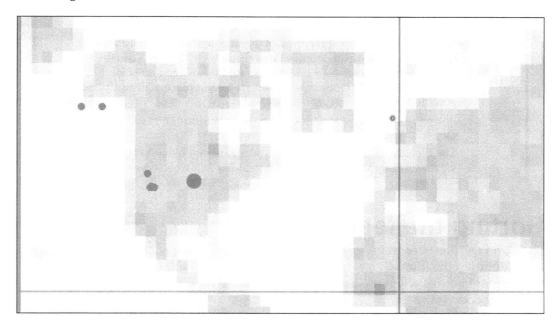

Once the application is compiled to JavaScript, the geolocation data is made available with user permission and the blue dot indicates the user's location, which in this instance is the relatively earthquake-free United Kingdom.

The Dart VM that runs in the command line and Dartium is not the only manifestation. The Dart team is working on two experimental versions of Dart in other contexts that vary significantly from the main Dart VM. Currently, both operate in a mobile context and focus on concurrency and high performance.

Fletch runs on desktop OSs, but is intended for Android and iOS execution with no JIT. Fletch takes a somewhat opposite approach to the highly asynchronous Dart, favoring user-level threads that are blocked but holding onto just a few resources. Fletch offers an interesting prospect for sharing the same code on different platforms; this would be a major productivity boost for mobile developers.

`https://github.com/dart-lang/fletch`

Sky is Android, only at the time of writing, and ambitiously aims to have highly responsive applications running at 120FPS. To achieve this, it prioritizes the user interface so that it can keep an 8ms response even when other processing is taking place. Currently, it can potentially run wherever the Dart VM can.

`https://github.com/domokit/sky_engine/tree/master/sky/packages/sky`

The Fletch and Sky prototypes, if successful, are likely to be mobile or server virtual machines and not embedded in a web server.

Sorting the feature list

So far, no use has been made of the third piece of data in the coordinates list, which is the depth of the quake. This data will be presented in the form of a sorted list of the current features when the user presses the **Sort** button. Let's have a look at the following code snippet:

```
void sortFeatures(Event evt) {
  featPlotter.sortFeatures();
  DivElement out = querySelector('#depthDetail');
  out.nodes.clear();
  featPlotter.geoFeatures.forEach((feature) {
    LIElement detail = new LIElement();
    detail.innerHtml = "${feature[5]}km - ${feature[3]}";
    out.nodes.add(detail);
  });
}
```

The list of features is sorted in the method `sortFeatures`, and as Dart knows nothing of the meaning of the contents of the list, we provide a comparator function that decides which feature is deeper by comparing the depth measurement held at index 5 of the list:

```
List sortFeatures(){
  geoFeatures.sort( (a,b) => a[5] - b[5] );
  return geoFeatures;
}
```

The comparator receives two arguments and returns 0 for items that are equal, a negative integer if `a` is less than `b`, or a positive integer if `a` is greater than `b`. Let's have a look at the following screenshot:

The depths are sorted in ascending order and presented as a simple bulleted list together with the location information.

Documenting Dart code with dartdoc

Documentation is a critical part of software development, and to encourage good documentation of packages, Dart has the tool `dartdoc` (`https://github.com/dart-lang/dartdoc/`), which creates static HTML documentation based on specially formatted code comments. Previous documentation tools for Dart were part of the SDK, while `dartdoc` is a separate project developed by the Dart team.

It can be installed using `pub` at the command line:

```
pub global activate dartdoc
```

We will take a look at a Dart package project to explore the features of `dartdoc`. Open the project `quakerecord` in the WebStorm Editor, and take a look at the file `quakerecord.dart`:

```
library quakerecord;
export 'src/quakerecord_base.dart';
```

This package exports a single file, `quakerecord_base.dart`, and in this file, the class `Processor` is declared:

```
/// A lightweight object to process a raw earthquake feature.
///
/// * Must have valid JSON.
/// * Must be less than 128MB.
///
class Processor {

  // Store for the JSON.
  String _feature;

  /// The state of processing
  bool get processed => true;

  /// The default constructor.
  ///     Processor processor;
  ///     processor = new Processor('{}');
  Processor(String feature) {}

  /// Returns a converted object based on the feature passed into
  /// the constructor [Processor].
  object convert() {
    // A normal comment.
```

```
    return new Object();
  }

  /// Changes feature based on partial data.
  /// *BETA QUALITY*
  ///
  /// 1. Estimates end points.
  /// 2. Transforms polarity.
  ///
  void experimentalNewMethod() {}
}
```

Note the use of the /// triple slash comment style — this is what dartdoc is looking for. The class declaration comments contain an unordered list *, the constructor has a section of sample code, the convert method has a link [] declared to the constructor, and experimentalNewMethod has a numbered list and formatting.

> For full details of Dart comments and documentation guidelines, see:
> https://www.dartlang.org/articles/doc-comment-guidelines/

There is also an additional class called ProcessHelper in recordhelper.dart:

```
/// A helper class to deal with quake feature settings.
class ProcessHelper {

  ///Swaps the data structure.
  void reversePolar() {}
}
```

To transform the comments into a web page, run dartdoc on the folder containing pubspec.yaml:

```
~/quakerecord/$ dartdoc
Generating documentation for 'quakerecord' into quakerecord/doc/api/
parsing lib/quakerecord.dart...
Parsed 1 file in 15.6 seconds.
generating docs for library quakerecord from quakerecord.dart...
Documented 1 library in 20.0 seconds.
Success! Open quakerecord/doc/api/index.html
```

A `doc` sub-folder is created in the project containing a folder named `api` that holds the documentation. Open the page in your favorite web browser and take a look at the output for the `Processor` class. Let's have a look at the following screenshot:

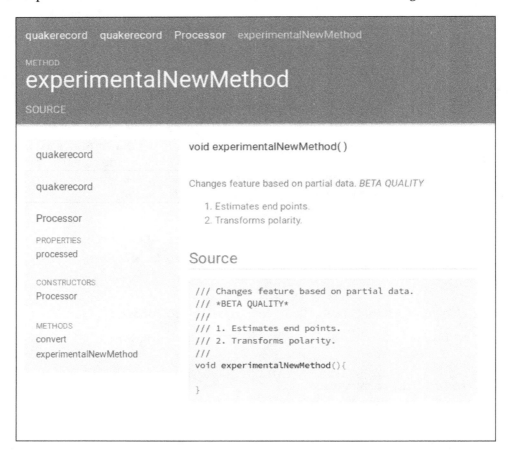

Finally, you may be wondering where the class `ProcessHelper` from `recordhelper.dart` is located on the generated page. It is not part of the documentation as it is not exported from the package, and because of this, is considered to be a private implementation detail that the consumer of the package does not need to know about.

Summary

We have seen how visualization can be made from raw data and rendered in animated form with a client using the HTML5 canvas. This can also be made interactive with popups and zooming facilities.

HTML5 can be used to provide desktop notifications and utilize the user's geolocation as part of the application. High quality formatted and standard documentation for the quake map viewer project was generated with the SDK tool `dartdocgen`.

We have explored data structures and had a look at convenient sorting and iterating facilities.

Moving on from this project, the data can still be presented in a more detailed manner across a date range. We will look at how Dart can be used to build a staple of businesses and other applications — printable reports. Also, we will build upon the API to allow direct entry of geographical information rather than relying on an external data feed.

10
Reports and an API

Man is still the most extraordinary computer of all.

– John F. Kennedy

A report is a common output of computer systems no matter what the application type, be it a business application or a game. Although alerts, dashboards, and widgets have been developed for decades, they do not seem able to compete with the effectiveness of a report, which has a defined scope (for example, the previous six weeks of data) and can be converted into and executed in many other document formats on other devices.

The digestion of data output from computer systems still has a human factor, even though computers have advanced a lot since the days of U.S. President Kennedy. You may wonder how long it will be before the insight of an expert is matched by a big data analysis or genuine **Artificial Intelligence (AI)**.

An API is a common feature of applications, especially those that are in a cloud that expands the usefulness of a system and drives the integration.

Recapping the earthquake system

The earthquake monitoring system will be further explained in this chapter. This time, the REST API will be expanded to add new data from another source, and a website will be created in order to provide a user interface for report generation. The API-accepting input opens up a wider variety of data sources, including the generated test data for development environments.

The reports will primarily be in HTML format, all though we will also look at other formats. The **Comma-separated Values (CSV)** format continues to persist as a user requirement on most systems, simply because it is flexible and easy to use in a spreadsheet and in other applications. Let's take a look at how the API client and reporting fit into the overall system:

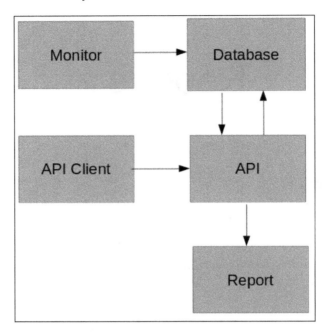

This project will have many parts when completed, which is typical of many systems. Not to scare any new programmers, but this is actually a fairly simple system. If you don't believe me, consider a modern social network website that receives text, photographs from many sorts of device, and API clients. Now imagine the number of subsystems and management reports it would require!

Advancing the REST API

This API will be far more useful and will provide us with the ability to add data so that the current web data feed is not the only data source.

The sample code in the `georestwebservice` project (of this chapter) is an updated version of the API with the new `recordFeature` method in the `georestwebservice.dart` file:

```
@ApiMethod(path: 'record', method: 'POST')
QuakeResponse recordFeature(QuakeRequest request) {
  DaoQuakeAPI quakeAPI = new DaoQuakeAPI();
  quakeAPI.recordFeature(getFeatureAsJSON(request));

  QuakeResponse quakeResponse = new QuakeResponse();
  quakeResponse.result = "1";

  return quakeResponse;
}
```

This method will use the standard HTTP POST verb in order to receive the input from the client application. As the `rpc` package wraps the entire method and composes and sends error responses, there is no need for error handling in this method. If, for example, something goes wrong while storing a result in the database, the client will receive an error message.

The following `getFeatureAsJSON` function, that is found in the `helpers.dart` file, converts the incoming `QuakeRequest` object into a JSON string:

```
String getFeatureAsJSON(QuakeRequest request) {
  String feature = jsonData;
  feature = feature.replaceAll("MAG", request.magnitude.toString());
  feature = feature.replaceFirst("TIME", request.time.toString());
  feature = feature.replaceFirst("LAT", request.latitude.toString());
  feature = feature.replaceFirst("LONG", request.longitude.
toString());
  return feature;
}
```

The jsonData string is a template for the GeoJSON feature. The String class has numerous useful methods that are used to match strings, and these are used to generate the final string that is returned from the function. The replaceAll method is used to replace every occurrence of a string; in this case, for the magnitude that appears as a value and in the text description. The replaceFirst method is used to replace the first occurrence of a string and is used in this function for the values that appear only once in the string.

The following API method's parameter is a simple class that is declared in the same file that contains four fields:

```
class QuakeRequest {

  @ApiProperty(required: true)
  int time;

  @ApiProperty(required: true)
  double magnitude;

  @ApiProperty(required: true)
  double longitude;

  @ApiProperty(required: true)
  double latitude;
}
```

The fields are annotated, which allows the rpc package to handle the marshaling of data through the REST interface.

Passing parameters to the API

One method of providing input to a REST API is via the calling URL, and this will be used to get a specified number of entries from the database using the following URL:

```
http://127.0.0.1:8080/api/quake/v1/recent/100
```

The implementation involves extending the pattern of the path with a curly bracket syntax (these correspond to the String parameters in the function):

```
@ApiMethod(path: 'recent/{count}')
Future<List<String>> recent(String count) async {
  DaoQuakeAPI quakeAPI = new DaoQuakeAPI();
  return await quakeAPI.fetchRecent(int.parse(count));
}
```

The int.parse method is used to convert the count string into a database query parameter.

Posting on the API

In the georestwebservice project in this chapter, the source code is an updated version of the API with the new recordFeature method in the daoapi.dart file, which is as follows:

```
Future<List<String>> recordFeature(String json) async {
  var dbConn;
  DateTime time = new DateTime.now();
  String featureID = time.millisecondsSinceEpoch.toString();
  List<String> result = new List<String>();

  try {
    dbConn = await connect(uri);

    await dbConn.execute(
        'insert into dm_quakefeatures (qufeat_id, geojson) values (@
qufeat_id, @geojson)',
        {'qufeat_id': featureID, 'geojson': json});
  } catch (exception, stacktrace) {
    print(exception);
    print(stacktrace);
  } finally {
    dbConn.close();
  }
  result.add(featureID);
  return result;
}
```

This method will create a featureID string for the incoming feature's details, which is then inserted in to the dm_quakefeatures table together with the supplied data from the client. The generated featureID string is then returned to the calling application for future reference.

Connecting to an API client

The client will be a command-line application that is used to add new features to the database using the new REST API method.

This project is a command-line application and uses the dart:io package, which has similar functionality to dart:html to work with an HTTP request, as shown in the following code:

```
main() async {
  print("API client");

  HttpClient client = new HttpClient();
  HttpClientRequest request = await client.postUrl(Uri.parse(apiUrl));
  request.headers.contentType = ContentType.JSON;
  await request.write(JSON.encode(getFeature()));

  HttpClientResponse response = await request.close();
  print("${response.toString()}");

  response.transform(UTF8.decoder).listen((contents) {
    request.close();
    print(contents);
    print("API client - done");
    exit(0);
  });
}
```

The application will post a single-feature JSON string to the API, wait for the response, display the response, and then exit. If multiple features are required, the program can simply be rerun.

Varying the data

The client will provide a generated feature to post to the API when it is run. Rather than having set data, a feature will be randomly generated. To generate random numbers in Dart, we can make use of the Random class from dart:math as follows:

```
Map getFeature() {
  var rng = new Random();
  var now = new DateTime.now();
  Map feature = new Map();
  feature['time'] = now.millisecondsSinceEpoch;
  feature['magnitude'] = rng.nextInt(8) + 1;
  feature['latitude'] = rng.nextDouble() * 90;
  feature['longitude'] = rng.nextDouble() * 90;
  return feature;
}
```

The Random class has methods to provide integer and double values, the former allowing the setting of an upper limit. The nextDouble method returns a value between 0 and 1, so this value can simply be multiplied by the maximum desired value. The time will be set to the current time.

The dart:math package contains a wide range of functions, and if you browse the documentation, you will see that most of the types are not integer or double, but number. In Dart, integer and double are the subtypes of a number object, and the number object implements the basic operators (+, *, / and so on).

The Dart specification contains arbitrary precision integers, which results in a difference in behavior between JavaScript and Dart compiled to JavaScript when dealing with very large numbers. This applies to numbers outside the -253 to 253 range, so this point is probably the only concern that we have for very advanced and unusual applications!

Returning to the map

To view the generated data, the quake map view from the previous chapter can be used. Let's have a look at the visual representation of the generated data in the following screenshot:

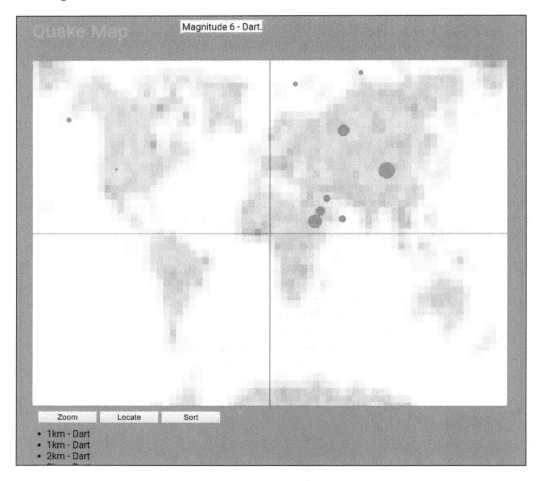

Once the command–line API client has been run a number of times, the map will soon be populated. Try adjusting the inputs for the generated data to cover more of the map, as the current numbers are skewed toward the top-right corner.

Reporting on the data

There are numerous existing systems that can be used to create reports, Microsoft **SQL Server Reporting Services (SSRS)**, that has a large install base. Due to Dart's support for the most ubiquitous formats, such as XML, and its ability to work with industry standard databases, solutions built with Dart can certainly be integrated.

The reporting feature that we will consider here is a pure Dart implementation. For many applications, reporting even a lightweight reporting feature and an export can greatly increase the usefulness. The added advantage here is the ease of deployment, even in enterprise situations.

The ReportSite project

Users will access the reports via a small website that will allow them to select each report type. This website is implemented in the `ReportSite` project, and the `main.dart` file sets up the initial page with event handlers for the button, as shown in the following figure:

The reports are filled with data from the REST API methods, so ensure that this is running if you wish to view reports. They are rendered in HTML and displayed on the same web page. The following excerpt from the `report_latest.dart` file shows how this is implemented:

```
querySelector('body').setInnerHtml(rep.output.toString(),
treeSanitizer: new ReportSanitizer());
```

This is a straightforward method call with the HTML string for the page, so why is a second parameter required? This is a security measure to ensure that the user-supplied content does not claim any undesired HTML string or script when being rendered in the display. Consider the following code snippet:

```
class ReportSanitizer implements NodeTreeSanitizer {
  void sanitizeTree(Node node) {}
}
```

The `ReportSanitizer` class is a **No Operation (NOP)** implementation, as the HTML is known to be from a trusted source.

Report classes

A report is made of a series of objects in a list, and the page elements are to be based on a similar interface so that the new page elements can be added to the package without having to change the display or export functions.

The page elements are implemented in the `report_elements.dart` file, which is part of the `reports` package project.

The core class will be called `Element`, and as it is to be used as an interface for other classes, it will be declared as follows:

```
abstract class Element {
  void setContent(var content);
  String toHtml();
}
```

This class is declared as `abstract` and provides no implementation for the methods.

To demonstrate this, we will consider the `Title` page element class, which implements the element (the methods have the `@override` annotation, which provides feedback to code analysis tools and other developers that the method is an implementation of a base class) as follows:

```
class Title implements Element {

  String content;

  Title(this.content) {}

  @override
  void setContent(var content) {
    String input = content.toString();
    content = input;
```

```
    }

    @override
    String toHtml() {
      return "<h1>$content</h1>";
    }

}
```

If a method is not provided an implementation, then the Dart analyzer will warn you of 'Missing concrete implementation'.

The other core page elements follow the same pattern. To create a report, only a few lines of code are required, which are as follows:

```
var rep = new Report('Sample');
rep..addSection(new Title("Sample Report"))
    ..addSection(new Paragraph("This is a paragraph"))
    ..addSection(new Pagebreak())
        ..addSection(new Paragraph("This is a paragraph too"));
```

The Report object can be found in the reports_base.dart file in the Reports project, with its most important generate method being generated. This method iterates all the page element objects to build up the HTML report that is stored in the output field, as follows:

```
    bool generate() {
      output = new StringBuffer();
      allContent.forEach((content){
        output.write( content.toHtml() );
      });
      generatedTimestamp = new DateTime.now();
      return true;
    }
```

A StringBuffer object is used to build up the HTML report. This class is more efficient than appending a number of strings.

Strings are stored internally as an immutable format in Dart (as in most programming languages), and updating a string really entails building an entirely new string object. The StringBuffer object only creates a String object when the toString method is called.

Creating a printable report

The data is retrieved from the REST API and displayed in a tabular fashion by using the HTML `Table` element. In the `performLatest` method, JSON is retrieved from the web service using the following URL:

```
http://127.0.0.1:8080/api/quake/v1/recent/100
```

This returns a JSON list of the requested length (or less, if the database does not have sufficient records), as shown in the following code snippet:

```
[
  "{\"properties\":{\"mag\":1.04,\"place\":\"3km SSW of San
Bernardino, California\",\"time\":1440707640360,\"updated\"
:1440707771997,\"tz\":-420,\"url\":\"http://earthquake.usgs.gov
/earthquakes/eventpage/ci37234439\",\"detail\":\"
http://earthquake.usgs.gov/earthquakes/feed/v1.0/
detail/ci37234439.geojson\",\"felt\":null,\"cdi\":null,
\"mmi\":null,\"alert\":null,\"status\":\"automatic\",
\"tsunami\":0,\"sig\":17,\"net\":\"ci\",\"code\":\"37234439\",
\"ids\":\",ci37234439,\",\"sources\":\",ci,\",\"types\":\",
general-link,geoserve,nearby-cities,origin,phase-data,
scitech-link,\",\"nst\":27,\"dmin\":0.09553,\"rms\":0.11,
\"gap\":62,\"magType\":\"ml\",\"type\":\"earthquake\",
\"title\":\"M 1.0 - 3km SSW of San Bernardino,California\"},
\"geometry\":{\"type\":\"Point\",\"coordinates\":[-
117.30233,34.1023331,10.84]}}",
  ...
```

Once the data is retrieved, the report's element objects are created and the HTML for the report details are inserted as a paragraph by using the following code:

```
    ...
    String json = await HttpRequest.getString(jsonSrc);
    List<String> items = JSON.decode(json);
    DateTime dt = new DateTime.now();

    Report rep = new Report('Latest');
    rep
      ..addSection(new Title("Latest Quake Data Report"))
      ..addSection(new Paragraph(
          '<div style="align:center"><img src="img/logo.png"/></div>'))
      ..addSection(new Paragraph("Report Generated At : ${dt}"))
      ..addSection(new Pagebreak());

    var table = buildFeatureTable(items);
    rep
```

```
    ..addSection(new Paragraph('<table id="reporttable">' + table +
'</table>'))
    ..addSection(new Pagebreak())
    ..addSection(new Notes("Looks like a busy day!"))
    ..generate();
...
```

The `buildFeatureTable` loops over the incoming JSON data to create the rows for the table, as shown in the following screenshot:

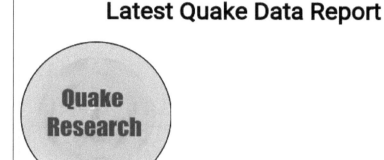

Latest Quake Data Report

Report Generated At : 2015-08-01 16:51:20.045

Type	Time	Place	Magnitude
earthquake	2015-07-28 19:12:04.535	Dart	4
earthquake	2015-07-28 19:12:03.051	Dart	6
earthquake	2015-07-28 19:12:01.735	Dart	2
earthquake	2015-07-28 19:12:00.253	Dart	2
earthquake	2015-07-28 19:11:58.750	Dart	3
earthquake	2015-07-28 19:11:57.152	Dart	5
earthquake	2015-07-28 19:11:53.941	Dart	1

The report is displayed in a continuous manner on screen. Switching to the print preview will show the page breaks between the sections that are created using **Cascading Style Sheets (CSS)**. The `div` element is added to the report with the `page-break-after:always` style by the `Pagebreak` page element.

Charting the data

A good visualization can make a great deal of difference to the person analyzing the data. To achieve this, we can use the modern_charts package, which provides a range of chart options. The chart report is implemented in the report_chart.dart file in the ReportSite project.

This chart will be based on the 20 most recent entries to the earthquake database using the following URL:

```
http://127.0.0.1:8080/api/quake/v1/recent/20
```

The first step to create a chart is to build up a dataset from the incoming JSON string as follows:

```
List dataset = [['Place', 'Magnitude']];

items.forEach((String featureJSON) {
  Map feature = JSON.decode(featureJSON);
  String place = feature['properties']['place'];
  place = place.substring(place.lastIndexOf(",") + 1);

  if (place.length > 5) place = place.substring(0, 5) + ".";
  var mag = feature['properties']['mag'];
  dataset.add([place, mag]);
});
DataTable table = new DataTable(dataset);
```

The first item in the dataset contains the number and names of the series to be plotted. The place name is processed so that the long and specific place names can fit on the axis of the chart. It is then added to the list with the magnitude, as shown in the following code:

```
Map options = {
  'colors': ['#3333cb'],
  'series': {'labels': {'enabled': true}}
};
```

The options object contains a range of details for the plotting of the chart, as follows:

```
DivElement container = new DivElement();
container
  ..id = "chartContainer"
  ..style.width = "90%"
  ..style.height = "90%";
```

```
var Title = new HeadingElement.h1();
Title.text = "Quake Chart";
document.body.nodes
  ..clear()
  ..add(Title)
  ..add(container);

LineChart chart = new LineChart(container);
chart.draw(table, options);
```

Once the dataset is ready, the HTML elements for the page can be put together, and the LineChart object that is created is given a reference to the object to add it on the page; in this case, a div element container (refer to the modern_chart package documentation for complete details).

The output of the previous code is shown in the following chart:

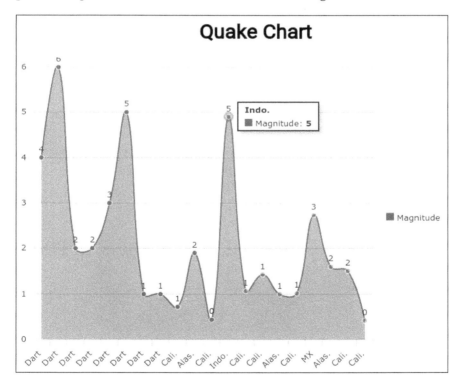

You may find working in Dartium to be an odd experience. It is a good browser, but you may prefer your daily web browser, such as Internet Explorer, Firefox, or Chrome, with your carefully-managed settings and collection of extensions. Using **Dart-to-JavaScript (dart2js)** before testing on other browsers interrupts the edit and refresh cycle. Ideally, Dart would run in any web browser.

Dartium is still going to be around for a long time; however, there is a project underway by the Dart team called the Dart development compiler. This new compiler has two goals, the first being to allow a smooth edit and refresh development experience on all browsers. A modular (incremental) compilation is used to aid a fast edit/refresh cycle. Find out more about the compiler project at `https://github.com/dart-lang/dev_compiler`.

The second goal of the compiler is to create a human-readable JavaScript format so that the output can easily be debugged. Initially supporting subset of the Dart language that is statically type checked. The type system has a different approach to dart2js that is to allow more direct and readable mapping of the Dart language to JavaScript. If you are developing in Firefox, then you will want to be able to debug your Dart code in it so that you do not have to step through the obfuscated code.

Exporting to CSV

CSV is a format that just keeps going thanks to its easy import into spreadsheets. The implementation of this report is found in the `report_csv.dart` file, and it retrieves the 50 most recent entries using the following URL:

```
http://127.0.0.1:8080/api/quake/v1/recent/50
```

CSV is a text format, and the fields are cleared of any comma characters so as not to have extra delimiters.

Let's consider the following code:

```
performExport(MouseEvent event) async {
  String json = await HttpRequest.getString(jsonSrc);
  List<String> items = JSON.decode(json);
  String csvexport = "Type, Time, Place, Magnitude\r\n";

  items.forEach((String featureJSON) {
    Map feature = JSON.decode(featureJSON);
    String type = feature['properties']['type'];
```

```
    String place = feature['properties']['place'];
    var mag = feature['properties']['mag'];
    var time =
        new DateTime.fromMillisecondsSinceEpoch(feature['properties']
['time']);
    String row = "$type, $time, ${place.replaceAll(",","")}, $mag\
r\n";
    csvexport += row;
  });

  querySelector('body').setInnerHtml('<pre>$csvexport</pre>',
      treeSanitizer: new ReportSanitizer());
}
```

The plain text CSV is set on the page with a `<pre>` HTML tag to ensure that the web browser does not change the intended formatting.

Let's have a look at the following screenshot:

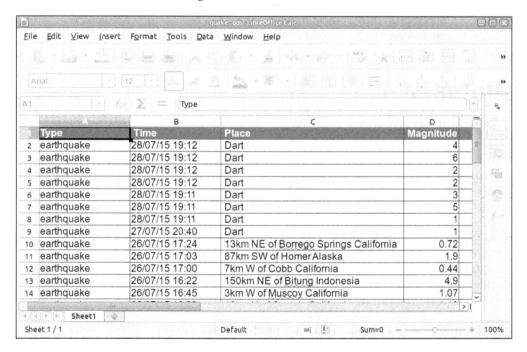

Exporting this data to a spreadsheet and applying some formatting produces a very usable result for further (human!) analysis.

You may already be aware of some of the existing JavaScript reporting libraries, such as jsPDF. If the reports package for the quake reports was developed further, could it be used by any web developer? One feature request that the Dart development team has received is the ability to create JavaScript libraries by using Dart. While this is possible by using the JavaScript interoperability, it is not easy to use and develop with Dart for this scenario.

The Dart development compiler is also being developed to allow the creation of JavaScript libraries that can be used seamlessly in non-Dart applications, where the use of Dart is an implementation detail that does not concern the consuming developer and application.

This will give Dart developers the ability to write first-class libraries that target both the Dart world and the larger JavaScript world, giving the library author a larger audience for their code. This also assists in integrating Dart into the existing code bases without transforming the entire project to a new language, which can be critical in risk-averse environments.

Summary

In these past few chapters we have built a powerful geographic application built on a real-world data source.

The API was expanded to provide data input using multiple methods with the powerful standard rpc package, and it continued to work with the relational database. The math package was used to generate a range of test data in order to push the limits of the application.

The reporting application shows how server–side Dart can be used to process and extract significant data in useful formats. We looked at how Dart can work with databases to produce reports in standard industry formats with the class and inheritance features of the language being used to build an object model for an extensible reporting system.

The continued development of the Dart language via the Dart development compiler may open further possibilities for web applications on the client side and also the server side. The Dart language can rapidly develop full-featured applications that can meet users' needs and provide a solid, dependable, and dynamic platform for developers.

Index

A

Angular
about 45
URL 45
Apache 113
API
connecting, to API client 204
data, charting 212-214
data, exporting to CSV 214-216
data, reporting 207
data, varying 205
generated data, viewing on map 206
posting on 203
printable report, creating 210, 211
report classes, using 208, 209
ReportSite project, creating 207, 208
Application Resource Bundle (ARB)
about 81
URL 81
args package
URL 41
Artificial Intelligence (AI) 199
async keyword 129
Atom Editor
about 6
URL 6
Audacity
about 89
URL 89
await keyword 129

B

Bfxr
about 88
URL 88
blog editor
about 115
blog, refreshing 120, 121
complex forms, handling 118
data, saving to disk 119
default graphic, serving 120
encryption 117
form, processing 118, 119
password, protecting 116
blog server
404 error, serving 104
about 95
blog posts format, storing 96
file, locating 103
folder of files, reading 98
HTTP protocol 95
images, serving 102
index page, rendering 101, 102
request, handling 98, 99
robots.txt 100
single blog post, rendering 100, 101
single image file, serving 103
starting up 96
text files, reading 97
text, serving 99, 100
browser
application, running 14-16

C

caching 121, 122
Cascading Style Sheets (CSS) 211
Chocolatey
  URL 5
class designer, dialog package
  adding 36
  class, constructing 37
  complicated dialog, building 36, 37
  events sequence 38
client application
  creating 169
  dates, formatting 172, 173
  grid, packaging 169
  grid view control, configuring 171
  JSON, fetching 170, 171
  page, displaying 175
  real-time updates, initiating 169, 170
  table, building 174
  time, formatting 172
  update, performing 170
command-line app, text editor
  canvas, using 43
  creating 38
  debugging 41
  file handling, with IO package 40, 41
  HTML5, using 43
  pie chart, drawing 44, 45
  project structure 39
  source code, processing 39
  statistics, integrating 43
command-line tools
  dart 8
  dart2js 8
  Dartanalyzer 8
  Dartdocgen 8
  Dartfmt 8
  pub 8
  reference link 8
  using 8
Comma-separated Values (CSV)
  about 200, 214
  data, exporting 214-216
comment style
  about 20
  references 20

cross-origin resource sharing (CORS) 127
CSS editor
  using 17
custom annotation
  creating 77, 78

D

Dart
  about 1, 24
  history 3
  PostgreSQL, using 141
  reference link 4
dart:math package 205
dartdoc
  URL 194
  used, for documentation 194-196
Dartium 15, 88
dartlang plugin
  about 6
  URL 6
Dartosphere
  URL 132
Dart SDK
  URL 107
Dart-to-JavaScript (dart2js) 45, 214
Dart VM
  code execution 35, 36
  multi-processing 36
  observing 151, 152
  URL 151
database
  data, saving 140
  PostgreSQL, using from Dart 141
database system
  installing 141
data collector application
  creating 157
  data, filtering 158, 159
  data maintenance, improving 160
  data table, adding 158
  executing 162
  feature, converting to JSON 160
  GeoJSON data collector, modifying 158
  single feature, storing 161
data monitor logging 139, 140
data source 136

intl package
  exploring 79
  language combo box, adding 84, 85
  language, modifying for user interface 83
  strings, extracting 80
  strings, locating for translation 79, 80
  translations text, integrating 83
IO package
  using 40, 41
iteration
  overview 177, 178

J

JavaScript
  about 2
  minified output, creating 47
  text editor, compiling 45, 46
JavaScript Object Notation (JSON)
  about 14, 126
  serving 127
JetBrains
  reference link 18
JSON feed
  consuming 127, 128
  generating 126

K

keyboard controls
  updating, for fullscreen mode 75, 76

L

language combo box
  adding 84, 85
LiveScript 2
load testing
  about 110
  load testing application, updating 132, 133
  simple load tool, building 110, 111
local package reference, dialog package
  About dialog box, defining 29, 30
  adding 27
  alert dialog box, defining 28
  base dialog box, defining 28
  confirmation dialog box, using 30

scope 28
word count, obtaining 31
word frequency, determining 32, 33
logging
  about 113, 138
  data monitor logging 139, 140
  example 138, 139
  logging package, URL 113
  request information, extracting 114, 115
  text files, writing 114

M

mapviewer project
  data, fetching 183, 184
  display, animating 181, 182
  display, zooming 187, 188
  map image, drawing 179
  map indicators, updating 184
  map, plotting 180
  mouse over popups, displaying 185-187
  overview 178, 179
Markdown
  URL 50
metadata
  adding 77
  custom annotation, creating 77, 78
  user interface text, translating 78, 79
mouse controls
  adding, for fullscreen mode 76
Multipurpose Internet Mail Extensions
    (MIME)
  about 100
  reference link 100
MySQL 140

N

named parameter
  versus optional positional parameter 70, 71
navigation, presentation application
  button key presses, handling 59
  Function type, using 60
  implementing 59
  max function, using 60
  min function, using 60
  slider control, using 61

Non-Sucking Service Manager (NSSM) tool
URL 109
using 109

O

object-orientated programming
reference link 24
optional positional parameter
versus named parameter 70, 71
Oracle 140
output folder
creating 130, 131

P

packages
importing 11
unwrapping 9
URL 10
pgAdmin GUI
about 142-144
command line arguments,
managing 148, 149
database, creating 145
database, maintaining 148
data, deleting 150
data, inserting 146, 147
data, retrieving 149, 150
login, creating 145
running 147, 148
table, defining 145, 146
URL 142
Polymer
about 45
URL 45
Pootle
URL 82
PostgreSQL
about 141
URL 141
using, from Dart 141
presentation application
building 49
bullet point slides, building 53
colors, modifying 64, 65
core classes, defining 56

current slide, displaying 59
data, transforming into HTML 57
date, adding 65, 66
event streams, listening 64
handout notes, adding 69
keyboard events, responding 62, 63
key help, displaying 63
launching 52, 53
laying out 50
mixin class, using 54-56
parsing 51
presentation, editing 58
presentation format, defining 50, 51
presentation, navigating 59
presentation, timing 66
project structure 52
sample presentation 52
visual overview, of slides 68, 69
private fields
accessing 54
getters, using 54
setters, using 54
pub
about 80
URL 80
Pubspec file
about 10
URL 10

R

Redstone
about 105
URL 105
REST
about 163
reference link 163
REST API
advancing 201, 202
parameters, passing 202
Rikulo
about 105
URL 105
robots.txt standard 100
rpc package
references 163
using 163

U

unit testing
about 152
test results, examining 156
tests, grouping 155
unit tests, running 153
unit tests, writing for data monitor 154
Unix
deployment 107
Uri (Uniform resource identifier)
property 99
user
location, plotting 190-192
notifying, for update 189, 190
user interface
language, modifying 83
text, translating 78, 79

V

variables
declaring 12

W

web interfaces
building 45

web scripting
history 2
web service
API, discovering 167, 168
API server, initiating 163, 164
creating 162
data, supplying 166, 167
error handling 165
executing 168
latest information, serving 166
methods, exposing 164, 165
rpc package, using 163
WebStorm IDE
about 5
downloading 5
features 6
URL 5

X

XML feed
generating 123, 124
RSS, serving 125

Y

Yet Another Markup Language (YAML) 10

Thank you for buying
Dart By Example

About Packt Publishing

Packt, pronounced 'packed', published its first book, *Mastering phpMyAdmin for Effective MySQL Management*, in April 2004, and subsequently continued to specialize in publishing highly focused books on specific technologies and solutions.

Our books and publications share the experiences of your fellow IT professionals in adapting and customizing today's systems, applications, and frameworks. Our solution-based books give you the knowledge and power to customize the software and technologies you're using to get the job done. Packt books are more specific and less general than the IT books you have seen in the past. Our unique business model allows us to bring you more focused information, giving you more of what you need to know, and less of what you don't.

Packt is a modern yet unique publishing company that focuses on producing quality, cutting-edge books for communities of developers, administrators, and newbies alike. For more information, please visit our website at www.packtpub.com.

About Packt Open Source

In 2010, Packt launched two new brands, Packt Open Source and Packt Enterprise, in order to continue its focus on specialization. This book is part of the Packt Open Source brand, home to books published on software built around open source licenses, and offering information to anybody from advanced developers to budding web designers. The Open Source brand also runs Packt's Open Source Royalty Scheme, by which Packt gives a royalty to each open source project about whose software a book is sold.

Writing for Packt

We welcome all inquiries from people who are interested in authoring. Book proposals should be sent to author@packtpub.com. If your book idea is still at an early stage and you would like to discuss it first before writing a formal book proposal, then please contact us; one of our commissioning editors will get in touch with you.

We're not just looking for published authors; if you have strong technical skills but no writing experience, our experienced editors can help you develop a writing career, or simply get some additional reward for your expertise.

Learning Dart

ISBN: 978-1-84969-742-2   Paperback: 388 pages

Learn how to program applications with Dart 1.0, a language specifically designed to produce better-structured, high-performance applications

1. Develop apps for the Web using Dart and HTML5.

2. Build powerful HTML5 forms, validate and store data in local storage, and use web components to build your own user interface.

3. Make games by drawing and integrate audio and video in the browser.

4. Learn how to develop an application with the help of a model-driven and fast-paced approach.

Mastering Dart

ISBN: 978-1-78398-956-0   Paperback: 346 pages

Master the art of programming high-performance applications with Dart

1. Improve the performance of your Dart code and build sophisticated applications.

2. Enhance your web projects by adding advanced HTML 5 features.

3. Full of solutions to real-world problems, with clear explanations for complicated concepts of Dart.

Please check **www.PacktPub.com** for information on our titles

Dart Cookbook

ISBN: 978-1-78398-962-1   Paperback: 346 pages

Over 110 incredibly effective, useful, and hands-on recipes to design Dart web client and server applications

1. Develop stunning apps for the modern web using Dart.

2. Learn how to store your app's data in common SQL and NoSQL databases with Dart.

3. Create state-of-the-art web apps with Polymer and Angular.

RESTful Java Web Services

ISBN: 978-1-84719-646-0   Paperback: 256 pages

Master core REST concepts and create RESTful web services in Java

1. Build powerful and flexible RESTful web services in Java using the most popular Java RESTful frameworks to date (Restlet, JAX-RS based frameworks Jersey and RESTEasy, and Struts 2).

2. Master the concepts to help you design and implement RESTful web services.

3. Plenty of screenshots and clear explanations to facilitate learning.

Please check **www.PacktPub.com** for information on our titles

www.ingramcontent.com/pod-product-compliance
Lightning Source LLC
Chambersburg PA
CBHW060541060326
40690CB00017B/3564